LEADING OUR WAY

LEADING OUR WAY

How Women Are Re-defining
Leadership

GAIA VAN DER ESCH

WILEY

This edition first published 2024

Gaia van der Esch©2024

Registered Office(s)

John Wiley & Sons Ltd, The Atrium, Southern Gate, Chichester, West Sussex, PO19 8SQ, UK
John Wiley & Sons, Inc., 111 River Street, Hoboken, NJ 07030, USA

Editorial Office

The Atrium, Southern Gate, Chichester, West Sussex, PO19 8SQ, UK

For details of our global editorial offices, customer services, and more information about Wiley products visit us at www.wiley.com.

Library of Congress Cataloging-in-Publication Data

Names: Esch, Gaia Van der, author.
Title: Leading our way : how women are re-defining leadership / Gaia van der Esch.
Description: Hoboken, NJ : Wiley, 2024. | Includes index.
Identifiers: LCCN 2023032190 | ISBN 9781394191819 (hardback) | ISBN 9781394232901 (adobe pdf) | ISBN 9781394232895 (epub)
Subjects: LCSH: Leadership in women.
Classification: LCC HQ1233 .E78 2024 | DDC 303.3/4082—dc23/eng/20230830
LC record available at https://lccn.loc.gov/2023032190

Cover Design: Wiley
Cover Image: © Daniil Khailo/Shutterstock
Author Photo: Courtesy of the Author

SKY10058973_110123

To the women of my family, who taught me kindness and courage, independence and empathy.
To you who is reading, with the hope that these values and this book can guide you in leading your way.

CONTENTS

CONTENTS

ACKNOWLEDGEMENTS

A HUGE THANK YOU GOES to Christiana, Gitanjali, Becky, Diane, Tawakkol, Comfort and Gloria (and to their teams!)—all of whom jumped on board this project with me. Thank you for believing in my vision, for sharing your stories and for inspiring us to lead our way. I insisted on having your names on the cover page, because this book is ours, not mine alone.

To the Wiley team—thanks for believing in this out-of-the-box project, and for giving me your full confidence and the freedom to build it and write it exactly as I wished to do.

I also want to say a big thanks to the army of people who helped make this book happen—friends, colleagues, university contacts, as well as some people I hardly knew. Thank you for believing in my idea, and for mobilising your social capital to get me the interviews behind this book. I was moved by the support I got throughout the process—it gave me the conviction and energy to overcome the challenges along the way, so your support was more precious than you can imagine.

Last but not least, I want to thank the people who stood by my side. My (in two days to be) husband (yes, my book deadline was the day before our wedding), my girlfriends, my family. Thank you for "volunteering" to be part of my mock interviews, for reading my chapters late into the night, for cheering me up when I was down, for celebrating with me every small achievement. A special mention goes to my dad, Stephen Andrew van der Esch, who—having just retired from his career in biology—became my "research assistant", helping me process the background info and prepare the interviews with the featured leaders. All of you, each in your own way, made it possible for me to write an entire book while being in a CEO role and planning a big Italian wedding. You are my rocks!

ABOUT THE AUTHOR

Gaia van der Esch is an Italian–Dutch CEO, policy expert and author, driving change and impact in the public and non-profit sectors.

Gaia is currently the managing director of a large foundation working on climate change, inequalities and civic participation across 50 countries. Prior to this appointment, she served as the G20 EMPOWER Sherpa under the G20 Italian presidency—leading the G20 private–public alliance for the advancement of women's leadership. Before this, Gaia spent 10 years working in Africa, the Middle East, Europe, and the USA—holding executive roles with international NGOs and think tanks. Because of her accomplishments, she was recognised by Forbes in its "30 Under 30 Europe List" (2017) and by Nova Talent as "Supernova of the Year" (2022).

As an executive and policy expert, Gaia is a contributor for several media outlets in Italy and internationally. Her first book, *Volti d'Italia*, was released in 2021—delving into polarisation and politics in Italy. She regularly intervenes as a speaker and expert at international events, and on television and radio.

Gaia holds a Bachelor of Philosophy from La Sapienza and two master's degrees: in International Relations from Sciences Po Paris and in Public Administration from the Harvard Kennedy School.

INTRODUCTION: WHY LEADERSHIP, AND WHY ME?

I WAS RAISED FREE.

Free to play, free to dream, free from roles, free to be and become myself.

How?

Imagine a medieval village on a hilltop, perched on a beautiful volcanic lake, surrounded by green hills, where kids are playing in the streets while old Italian grandmas sitting in the shadow of their doorsteps keep a discrete but constant eye on them.

I was one of those kids.

Used to living outside: be it running up and down the streets, swimming or fishing in the lake, pony riding at the local farm, learning how to use a bicycle on the only flat road along the lake—all while getting all sorts of scars and a variety of rare diseases from the stray cats we would try to cure.

Used to being independent: since age three, I was authorised to walk to the music school by myself—my parents knew there was a network of old ladies sitting by their windows keeping an eye on me; and soon after, I started my summer business to be able to afford candy supplies and gelato for the whole season—selling old books, pots and pans, or any object our neighbours were ready to let go of, to tourists.

Used to standing up for what was important to me, I was well known among the village mayors for bursting into their offices, hardly reaching the height of their desk, to share my lists of complaints—from broken swings to scooters speeding on the street where we were training our bicycle skills; and I was well known in school for standing up for stuff—be it a classmate, my weekly boyfriend, my little brother.

Being used to all of this seemed and came natural to me. But I realised with time that it wasn't a given.

It took granting me the freedom to try things out and do it my way; it took giving the support and the encouragement where guidance or confidence-building were needed; it took drawing clear red lines that I couldn't cross. Be it the square at the end of the historical centre where cars were allowed again to drive, be it certain words or behaviours that were simply not tolerated within the family, or the clear requirement to attend and do my best at what was important to my parents: school, music classes, sports and family events.

Of all things, though, what shaped me the most were the daily examples and reference points of how things were done and—even more—of how things could be done differently.

Both my parents came from outside this small village in the countryside of Rome. A Milanese mother and a Dutch–Canadian father, who both came to Rome with a biology scholarship, fell in love and decided to settle down in the village nearby the research centre—to build their life together.

A life which had to bridge not only their differences in culture but also their difference in roots as they emerged from two opposite worlds.

My Italian family still lives today in the (relatively poor) outskirts of Milan. They migrated there from other parts of the country because the local factory was giving houses with water and electricity to its workers, and they saw it as their chance of moving out of poverty. After living under the fascist regime; refusing to ever take the fascist party card; suffering hunger, cold, and bombardments; they succeeded in rebuilding their lives. By exiting the factory and making their dream jobs come true: for Gianna, my grandmother, a hairdresser saloon—which she ran out of their living room; for Tersilio, my grandfather, driving trucks. And by creating their most precious accomplishment: my mum.

The biggest dream and drive for all though was to give my mother what they never had: an education. My grandad died as my mum was in high school due to an unknown (back then) sickness, my grandma—supported however possible by her 10 sisters—increased her work hours, her number of clients, to be able to afford my mum's education. And my mother delivered: a degree in biology, a job in the capital city, a life living the unlived dreams of her parents.

Now imagine the opposite. That is my other half.

My Dutch grandad came from a banker's family; my Canadian grandma from a military doctor's one. After being part of the anti-Nazi resistance in the Netherlands and imprisoned for a

few years in Germany, Bastiaan—my grandad—graduated as a
lawyer and moved to London for his PhD in law. There, while
playing tennis at the university club, he met Patricia Anne
Margaret, my grandma, known as "PAM", who had recently
graduated from a posh all-girls university in the United States
and also freshly moved to London for her history PhD. A power
couple who lived an international and upper-class life, from The
Hague to Paris, from Luxembourg to Brussels—surrounded by
four children, nannies and cooks.

A life filled with wealth and purpose. Which wasn't—as for my
Italian family—giving their children a better life than their own,
as that wasn't even a faraway concern. It was, rather, leaving their
children a better world to live in. Bastiaan dedicated his life to
building the European project, advancing our collective values
of peace, freedom, democracy. PAM dedicated her life to finding purpose in all sorts of other ways—since, in those years,
wealthy women were highly discouraged from having a full-time
job. After publishing a few books, PAM spent her life teaching
English, visiting prisoners, founding the renowned International
Bazar in Luxembourg to create a culture of charity among the
upper class, founding and presiding over the Femmes d'Europe
(European Women) Association in Brussels to advance women's
rights and serving as a loyal member of her Quaker community—
fighting for peace and equality, in the streets, in op-eds, in her
own patriarchal family.

And this is how we get to me: a result of this improbable mix.

With a Canadian grandmother screaming at me because I
behaved in a too non-lady-like manner at the dining table (i.e.
eating eagerly, without leaving any trace of food ever being on
my plate) and an Italian one teaching me to eat and savour

every little piece of it—because I was lucky to not starve. With a mother for whom her job as a biologist and our little home by the lake was the ultimate success—given her modest roots— and a father for whom the same job and the same home were never enough—compared to his upper-class upbringing.

A mix which wasn't always easy to manage but which did give me a unique perspective on the world.

A father who—unlike most dads in the village and certainly unlike his own father—cooked for us, took us to school, invented magical evening stories, took us on birdwatching trips and used to be the only man attending parent–teacher meetings, showing us that being a dad starts at home and teaching me that parity can and must be expected; and a mother who worked late, became the main breadwinner and taught us that nothing counts as much as your independence, especially as a woman. Dutch grandparents who made us tour European cities and institutions to teach us that we all have a role to play in the greater good; our Italian grandmother who taught us the importance of family and the power of kindness and of modesty, especially in the smallest things we do—they reveal who you really are. A surname for which I was teased at school, teaching me it's never easy to be different, but which now gives me strength and uniqueness. A life in the calmness and isolation of a tiny village, regularly interrupted by jet-setting to see the family abroad. A mix and match of English, Italian, French, and even some Dutch, which trained my mind to think like a global citizen—without even realising it—while always staying rooted in the winding streets of my village.

An upbringing bridging worlds, cultures, social classes. An upbringing which shaped me to the core.

A bachelor's degree in philosophy and a master's in political science between Rome, Berlin, and Paris—filled with the hope they would give me the foundation to somehow contribute to our world. Taking on my first job as a humanitarian worker in the Middle East, to be there for those suffering due to absurd wars. After four years spent between Jordan, Iraq, Lebanon, and Turkey, moving to Geneva in a global executive role, aged 27, co-leading a large think-and-do-tank to ensure political and aid decisions were based on data, on reality, not on the usual poor planning and assumptions. Deciding to then return to study, this time in Boston, to get closer to the political world. Discovering, while there, my passion for writing. Returning, after 12 years abroad, to my home country, Italy, as a result of a mix of nostalgia and of my drive to contribute to its socio-political change—a return accelerated by the global pandemic and by my desire to be there, close to my parents, my grandmother, in the streets of my childhood. The publication of my first newspaper columns, then of my first book. Followed by an experience which changed my life trajectory more than I would have expected it to: being appointed as G20 Sherpa during the Italian presidency, leading the work of the G20 Alliance for the Empowerment and Progression of Women's Economic Representation (G20 EMPOWER).

Suddenly submerged in data, briefings, policies, reflections on gender inequality. And then having an eye-opening realisation: I had lived many of those data points, of those statistics, on my own skin; and, for the first time, I connected the dots—supported and encouraged by the amazing female colleagues that surrounded me—realising that such episodes, micro-aggressions, discriminations were linked to my gender, to being a woman. And that it wasn't just my problem, my challenge, my failure, but a systemic one.

Sexist comments, looks, gestures—be it at work, in the streets, while at the doctor; salary discrepancies, out-of-place questions on when I'll have kids; men struggling to accept me as their boss, undermining me whenever I succeeded. Some other men and women, luckily, teaching me, on the contrary, how to believe in myself, deal with such backlash, and leverage my management role to lift others up. But as all of this was happening, the good and the bad, I was naively oblivious of the fact that what I was seeing were not isolated accidents but symptoms of a system that needed rethinking, fixing, transformational change. Blissfully unaware of the fact that I was dealing with a systemic problem. A problem which, once I saw, I could no longer unsee.

One out of three women in the world has been a victim of physical or sexual violence. A total of 90% of the CEOs of the 500 largest American companies (Fortune 500) and 89% of heads of states worldwide are men. Women took on three times more unpaid child-caring work than men during the pandemic, a trend which simply reflects the pre-pandemic reality. And, according to the World Economic Forum, it will take another 131 years before we reach gender equality. I won't see it, my potential daughter will not see it, maybe—if we are lucky—my granddaughter could. . . this is the gravity of the situation.

Suddenly, everything my mum, my grandmothers had taught me—as a little girl—made sense.

At age seven, I managed to convince my parents (and my brother, as there was a requirement for us to do the same sports for logistical reasons) to enter us into figure skating. After karate, swimming, tennis, I could finally do a "girly" sport. My real objective? Wear—just as the girls I saw on television—a short and tight dress for the final show and have my hair and make-up done. That was my end-goal, my dream come true. This is why I remember, as if it was yesterday, the moment our teacher showed my mum the pictures of the sexy dresses she was meant to buy and asked her to free up her time to do my hair and make-up on the day. I was sitting on the side, trying to capture my mum's reaction, because I knew she wasn't the make-up and sexy pink dress type of mum—praying she would make an exception. "Is this the type of woman you want our daughters to become?", says my mum to the teacher with a severe look on her face. "Well", she continues before the baffled teacher has a chance to answer, "it definitely isn't what I hope for my daughter, so there is no way I am going to dress her up as one of those sexy ladies on TV at age seven and make her think there is any value or ambition in that—because there is none, she is smart, she is independent, she is not going to be taught to be an object of our patriarchal society". That was it. My dream was broken. My mum said she will think of something appropriate for my age, came and picked me up and walked away.

On the day of the show, as all the other girls were sitting with their mums getting their hair and make-up done, I was sitting with my mum—who had freed up her time—to get me ready as well. But not as the sexy doll I wanted to be, rather as an Indian girl, wearing my mum's hippy long skirt as a dress, and a red dot between my eyes in honour of a country filled with great women who had liberated their nation. As if that meant anything to a seven-year-old Gaia, whose vision of success was dancing on a TV show.

Reading this, you must be part of one of two teams: team "poor girl" or team "go Anna Rosa (i.e. my mum)". I was team "poor girl", for a long time. But I must admit a conversion happened, yes—to team "go Anna Rosa", once I started seeing the systemic problem we live in. Because that decision she took made me sad, very pissed, yes, but taught me something. Gave me a red line of what I should not be aiming for in my life—not because it's not authorised but because I could do better than that. Gave me a signal of which values we should carry as mothers, as women, as people younger girls and boys are looking up to. And, above all, taught me that being different doesn't necessarily mean being excluded, rather it means being special.

As I was entering the skating stage, despite being the only one with a long skirt and a red dot on my forehead, I could still perform the moves I had learned (also, I can assure you, I understood in that moment why skaters wear short skirts—a consideration which hadn't passed through my mum's head), and I was still part of the overall choreography. The other kids thought my outfit was part of the show, it made me different, special, capturing the attention I wouldn't have had if I had have looked like every other girl. And despite being disappointed, upset, that I was different—because I was—I still survived it, and that's also a good lesson to learn early on: you can get through a skating show, through life, even if you don't always fit the mould.

Standing up for what I care about but also standing up for myself, by owning—not hiding—my diversity, became a crucial part of my daily life. Because each time we stand up for ourselves, we are standing up for all women and are helping change a system which is breaking too many of us. And we need more women and men doing just that: understanding the systemic aspect which I had also not seen for too long;

stand up for themselves and play their part to be the change we want to see.

But for such change to be effective, we need to go even one step further.

While I was leading negotiations, defining policies, hosting high-level events on women empowerment and leadership at the G20, I noticed what—according to me—were shortcomings of the change we were trying to bring.

A lot of our focus was on how to get women into decision-making rooms, around the table. Which policies to adopt, be it quotas, targets, incentives for companies, to increase the 10% of women CEOs or heads of states, which is crucial.

But we often forgot the other side of the coin: what we would do once we get to that table.

If I teach a little girl the rules of the game, once she wins and she dominates the rules, I can't expect her to change those rules to help other girls win. She won, by playing by the rules of the game—meaning that's all she knows—and she will think that others should do just the same. But we forget that the reason why women are not emerging is also because the rules of the game are made by and for men. More often than not, these rules define our strengths as weaknesses: be it collaboration, be it empathy, be it our capacity for long-term thinking, our prioritisation of the common good. Instead, they reward competition, assertiveness, short-term profit, self-interest. Creating biased (and unhealthy) reward mechanisms which have, slowly but surely, brought our companies, our countries, our world, to the state we are in now: never-ending wars, catastrophic consequences of climate change, deeply entrenched inequalities, and discriminations.

If we don't start changing the rules of the game, what is being rewarded, or discouraged, and how, we will just continue perpetuating this faulty system, which is breaking our world, and which is the source of discrimination, be it against women or the many minorities, at all levels of society.

So, yes, we must get women around the table, just as we must increase the representation of all types of diversity—be it age, ethnicity, sexual orientation. Because it's the right thing to do, but also because—as proven by data—it is the smart thing to do: companies with diversity in their executive level and in boards outperform companies led by less diverse teams (i.e. in today's world, only men). But we must also get women and men to think differently, to act differently, once they are sitting in that chair, and we must create a new generation of leaders which is playing by different rules of the game. By redefining what leadership means, how it acts and looks like, for us and for the generations to come.

This means starting to value different and new traits, to allow women to bring all of themselves in their jobs, at the decision-making tables, at home, and to liberate men from having to act "as men do", be it at work or at home. Because we are all capable of empathy, of collaboration, of pursuing the common good, of kindness—if only these behaviours would be encouraged and not seen as weaknesses. And because we all need to shift gears, in our families, in our communities, in our jobs—from the most junior to the most senior level—if we want to take our world, our countries, our companies in a better direction, for the sake of humanity and for the sake of our planet.

And the good news is that we all have the power to do just that. As citizens, as consumers, as employees, as executives. Because—as you will discover through the pages of this book—leadership is not a title, what is written on our office door. Leadership is the commitment that each of us makes to change what we think is wrong. In our home, in our community, in our school, in our company, in our country. It is every small or big gesture, action, word we take or say, which makes us actors for change, which makes us one of the people helping to revise and redefine the rules of a broken game.

So, how can we go to this next level, rethink what leadership means?

As I sat with this question, I thought back to my childhood, my life. Of what helped me expand my imagination, learn how things are done, but even more, how they could or should be done differently.

The answer was easy: examples.

My parents, my grandparents, my friends and family from different cultures and countries, my colleagues, my bosses, my mentors. But also movie characters, book protagonists, who helped me see and imagine a different world. Role models, whom I have learned from and with. And who have the power to open our minds, to give us confidence, to make us feel less lonely in our ups and downs, in our thirst and hope for change.

And this is the spirit you will find in each page of this book.

Where you will encounter seven women from across the world, who have marked their countries, their companies, their community—be it by leading revolutions or soccer teams, climate negotiations or fashion ventures, the feminist movement or peace deals, science experiments and innovation. But who, even more, have done so by being their true selves, by leading in their own way.

In each page, you will discover the life and leadership journeys of these iconic women, with all the challenges and vulnerabilities hiding behind the face of success. But, even more, you will discover their eagerness and their urgency in rethinking what leadership means and looks like—for them, and for each and every one of you reading these words.

And, as you advance through the pages, we will define—together—a new set of traits which can help expand our idea and vision on what leadership acts, thinks, and looks like—for women and for men. Because fitting the mould is not going to allow us to bring the change we all want and need.

We break this mould by starting with the power of *optimism*—as a philosophy of life for all those who want to fix things through action, and which drives the powerful leader that delivered the most historic climate agreement to date—*Christiana Figueres*. To then get into the importance of *curiosity*, a trait which we are often lacking in today's world and which we tend to lose as we move up the ladder, convinced we know it all. A trait which, on the contrary, is crucial to make us learn, improve, and become over time more effective change-makers, innovators, leaders. A trait which *Gitanjali Rao*, the first-ever Kid of the Year of *TIME* magazine, a young innovator and scientist, embeds in everything she does. And, yes, we need more compassion, empathy, optimism, curiosity, kindness in everything we do, but to go far, we also need something else: *consistency*. A trait which *Becky Sauerbrunn*, the captain of the US national football ("soccer", for Americans) team, has been training for decades now, and which helps us understand that we don't control everything that will happen in our lives but that we can control how we show up every single day—and that can make a huge difference in how we lead, where we go, and where we get to. You should trust her, as she has got a few world cups and Olympic medals under her belt. *Authenticity* is another trait which emerges throughout the book: being ourselves is what makes us unique, and doing what makes us unique, following that passion, is what gives us an edge, what makes us stand out in the crowd. *Diane von Furstenberg*, the iconic designer who created the wrap dress, shares how she's done that in her life and how others can and should do just the same. It will make you happier, it will make you more fulfilled, it will make you more impactful and effective in whatever you do with your life. But what is all of this for? Well, for *freedom*. Freedom to be who we are, freedom to do what we want to do, to follow our dreams without being held back—from social pressure, from discriminatory laws, from religion, from dictatorial regimes. And no one is better placed to speak of this, of freedom, than *Tawakkol Karman*—the woman who led a revolution in her home country, Yemen, and succeeded in overturning the dictator, reaffirming equality for all, despite the long road that still lies ahead for her country and for most countries in the world. No wonder she was awarded the Nobel Peace Prize for this accomplishment. But we won't be able to lead our world towards freedom without *integrity*. Without the capacity to be honest, be fair, be coherent, be principled, in how we treat others—be it our family, our community, at our workplace, or in decision-making rooms. *Comfort Ero*, the CEO of one of the most renown think tanks working on conflict prevention, shares with us what integrity means and why it is so essential to leadership. A leadership which, though, above all, will not succeed in changing the rules of the game until we shift one fundamental trait: seeing leadership no longer as hierarchy but as *circularity*. Co-constructing, co-leading, as a means of building a better society, a better world. A world in which leadership is no longer attachment to power, to self-interest, to short-term results, but in which leadership is circular, focused on the common good, on long-term well-being of us humans and of our planet. And no one is better placed than the trailblazing and iconic *Gloria Steinem*, known as the "mother" of the women's liberation movement, to share some wisdom on how we can transform this different concept of leadership into reality.

But one trait underlies this all, brings it all together: *empathy*. Its Greek root, ἐν + πάθος, means: "in suffering with", "in passion with". A concept which we explore in the conclusion, as the key which is allowing all these impressive women to lead change, as the key that allowed me to write this book and guides me in my job as an executive, as the key that will guide your leadership in the right direction for our world.

In short, get ready to discover a set of interviews that will make you laugh, cry, think, doubt, believe in yourself, act, to become the change you want to see. With a set of women to whom goes all my gratitude, for jumping on board this journey with me, to redefine leadership together, and to inspire and empower together all those reading—boys and girls, women and men—to lead, and to do so in their own way.

• 1 •

OPTIMISM
Christiana Figueres

*When I started thinking of this book, one thing I was certain about was that
I wanted women out of the box.Women who don't homologate, who are bold, have
the courage to fail and to speak about it, even to laugh about it.Women who are
outspokenly themselves, with all the imperfections that come with it and—exactly
because of that—have the power to inspire others.*

Christiana Figueres is all the above, and more.

SINCE A FEW MONTHS, wherever I go, I have Christiana in my ears.While walking to the supermarket, on a train ride, on my way to a meeting. I have become more and more an *aficionada* of her podcast—Outrage + Optimism. Through her stories, the anecdotes on climate change negotiations, the interviews with her always impressive guests, Christiana manages to inspire me, to make me think, learn, expand my views on our world. But more than that, she manages to give hope on a topic which typically brings us down: climate change. And that is what got me hooked.

The hope is in her voice. Upbeat, full of courage, optimism, always searching for solutions, nonetheless brutally honest, realistic. And that hope activates me. It has the power to make each and every one of us feel like an important and purposeful piece on our collective path to change, rather than an inter-changeable or useless part of a dysfunctional machine. It's the kind of attitude our world needs more of. And it's what makes Christiana one of the most iconic figures in the climate change space: "the woman behind the Paris Climate Agreement", "one of the top world diplomats on climate change", "the ray of hope in the fight against global warming".

No wonder that suddenly sitting opposite Christiana, hearing her familiar voice from just a few centimetres across the table, feels exciting and surreal. And a little intimidating. If you have listened to her, you know how persuasive she is as a speaker, how insightful she is when interviewing others . . . living up to her level is not the easiest of tasks.

"I have three parts to the interview", I explain to her, "*Lead, change, inspire. Lead,* to discuss your vision of leadership. *Change,* to discuss how you would like leadership to change. And *Inspire,* to discuss your personal story and—through that— encourage others to lead".

"Well . . ." Christiana answers with a kind smile on her face, "I don't know what the difference is between the three, for me they are the same. You wouldn't lead if not to change something, and you wouldn't change something without inspiring—they are intertwined".

We both laugh as in one second, she has upended my interview script—but she quickly starts speaking again, this time to reas- sure me: "they are interlinked, but don't worry, I see how you want to split things, so please go ahead".

After these initial few exchanges and laughs, we wonder if we might be disturbing those around us—we both have loud voices, and even louder characters. Not the most welcome combination for a traditional British business environment. Christiana lives in Costa Rica but has travelled to London for meetings. This is why we are sitting in the business centre of a hotel right next to the iconic Trafalgar square. It's a historical building: the wall and ceiling covered in dark wood, the floor of the typical British moquette. There are international news- papers lying around—*The Telegraph, The China Daily.* There is an old fireplace, a modern coffee corner, and some comfy sofa-chairs where we had just sat down with our afternoon tea.

To not disturb, we decide to move into one of the small meeting rooms and, before I have the time to do so, I see Christiana already up, carrying my stuff: my backpack, my cup of tea. I quickly pick up her coat and my portable recorder and follow her into the meeting room. She is down to earth, she is kind, caring—my pre-existing admiration is reinforced by this initial impression and by each of her gestures.

"So, let's start", I say while pulling my chair closer to hers. Christiana looks straight into my eyes, pulls her chair closer to mine, and in her upbeat voice, answers, "Yes, let's go!"

INTERNAL COMMITMENT: HOW LEADERSHIP IS BORN

We delve right into the gist of the topic, leadership.

"Well, let me start by saying what leadership is not", says Christiana. "It is not whatever you have on your business card, nor your title, or what is written on your office door. It is not about a position, be it elected or nominated. It's about how you see yourself in the world with respect to change. And that is an internal commitment, which does not necessarily need you to be occupying particular positions. We are all in roles, in positions, whichever they are in our lives—and we can either decide to lead from there, as the centre of concentric circles that generate change, or we can choose not to, and just go with the flow. So, if you choose to dedicate time, energy, space, to make a difference, no matter your position, then—by definition—you are leading. This means we can all lead from where we are. When people assume their title alone entitles them to be 'a leader', it always makes the alarm bell in my head go off very loudly" she says, laughing.

"Are those leaders mainly men?" I ask to tease her.

Christiana stops laughing, and with a reflective look, seems to take a step back in her mind. "Well, I don't want to fall into simplistic ways of thinking. Yes, I would say it's mainly men, but statistically, historically, we have had more men leaders than women leaders, so maybe it's simply because they are statistically more present. I am actually grateful today to work with many men who do not fall into that simplistic box and who lead through their actions, not because of their titles. But yes, I think we are observing a more feminine trait that is emergent in both men and women, a trait that allows us to see the capacity to lead without a position and without a title. Is that a feminine trait? Probably. Is it a good trait that we should see more of? Definitely. I can tell you though from my experience, within the United Nations, within state diplomacy, that leadership in today's world is still seen as hierarchy—and that needs to change", she adds in a calm and serious tone.

"But I want to add something, a personal reflection: even while operating within this hierarchical and male-dominated leadership structure, I believe I stayed authentic, true to myself. I felt pretty comfortable in my skin in all the positions I held, be it as a negotiator for Costa Rica, the executive secretary of the United Nations Framework Convention on Climate Change (UNFCCC), or a corporate board member. I feel comfortable with myself, while at the same time, I am committed to bringing change, creating a different world. And I don't honestly ever remember thinking that in order to make a difference, I had to fit in that leadership mould, that I had to fulfil this or that expectation. Now that I think of it", she adds while still reflecting about the issue, "I don't remember ever having an outside reference dictating what

I am doing. My references are internal. Where do I feel I am being most authentic? What is deeply true for me? What is my grounding? What do I believe in? What are the skills that I can bring to this situation? I think this is how I managed to navigate the hierarchical leadership system—by not looking to the outside to define my actions, but rather looking inside for guidance. And I combined this inward-looking reference with pragmatism. I never saw myself with that title: "leader". I just knew there was a task to be done, a problem to be fixed. And I brought it my all, whether I was the best person for that task or not—and frankly, the moment you are given the task, that question becomes irrelevant. This is the task, you are the person facing it, so the only thing you can do is to go for it, and that's what I did—just as my parents taught me to", she adds with a proud look.

LA LUCHA SIN FIN OR THE ENDLESS STRUGGLE

Christiana comes from a privileged background. Her father, José María Hipólito Figueres Ferrer, was president of her home country, Costa Rica—serving at three different times between 1948 and 1974. Her mother, Rita Karen Olsen Beck, born in Denmark, became a Danish American-Costa Rican diplomat, social worker, and politician, in addition to serving as first lady during the presidencies of Christiana's father.

"My dad was a *huge* figure in my life", explains Christiana, underlining her father's immense influence on her. "I never related to him as daughter to father, because he wasn't a father, he was a public figure—also at home. And the values and principles he was guided by, the challenges and the struggles he fought through, are all running deeply through my veins—even today".

Christiana's father became president for the first time after winning the 1948 Civil War in Costa Rica. And, once in power, he took transformative decisions for his homeland. Besides writing a forward-looking constitution, he granted women the right to vote and Costa Rican nationality to those of African descent—which had been so far excluded from citizens' rights; and he abolished the army—a decision that makes Costa Rica even today one of the few countries in the world without a standing military force.

"You know", she says with a smile, "I'll tell you something that says it all . . . He founded a farm in Costa Rica and called it *La Lucha Sin Fin* [the endless struggle]. That was his philosophy of life: we will always have more to do, meaning it is impossible to get at some stage in life and think 'I am done'. If you win a battle, look for the next battle. If you don't win the battle, go back and find a way to win that battle. For my father, life was a struggle without end—and I completely buy into that. I live by that motto: trying to fix one problem, and then another, and then another".

"What about your mother?" I ask. "Well, my mother was a very tough mother. My brothers and sisters would agree that we grew up very much without mother's love or father's love, but with huge personalities who dedicated their lives to social justice—including my mother. She engaged in addressing racial inequalities, environmental issues. And from the minute we were born, both my parents were clear, firm, on one thing: the privilege my siblings and I grew up with was a privilege we were expected to use in service of others, of a bigger cause". As she speaks about her parents, I see deep respect in her eyes. "They were without question the people who inspired me, who instilled social justice in my DNA".

"I work on climate change because it is the mother of all injustices: there is injustice between the Global North and Global South; there is injustice between human beings currently alive and future generations; there is injustice from a gender perspective, men's decisions impacting women's lives more severely—as proven by numerous studies; there is injustice between those who have financial resources, education, who pollute but can also adapt better, and those who have less financial resources or education, who don't pollute but will struggle to adapt to the consequences of climate change; and, let's not forget, there is injustice between humans and other living species: we humans did this, the other species pay the price. It is all just unjust, hugely unjust, in whatever way you look at it", says Christiana, in an outraged voice. "So yes, climate change is the mother of all injustices, and I cannot imagine, now at 66, another battle I would have wanted to dedicate my energies, my life to. I also can't imagine another field equally frustrating and motivating with respect to doing something about social justice, and that is what drives me every single day".

Little did Christiana know that this passion for social justice, translated into an unstoppable drive for halting climate change, would bring her one day all the way to the helm of the climate change negotiations and lead her to be known as the intergovernmental leader behind the success of the Paris Agreement reached during the 21st Conference of the Parties (COP21), which convened in 2015. An agreement which, for the first time ever, saw almost all the world's nations support a common strategy to cut greenhouse gas emissions, to halt global warming. A commitment which, just a few years before, had been impossible to reach as part of the 2009 COP15 in Copenhagen.

"How did you manage to bring a whole intergovernmental system, that had failed just a few years before in Copenhagen, to deliver such a ground-breaking agreement? How did you break the unconstructive dynamic that had led to one failure after the other in global climate change diplomacy? Was it your attitude? Was it your behaviour with your team and then their attitude with others? Was it specific consultation processes and how you built them? Or just a convergence of government interests? What was it?" I flood Christiana with questions. She smiles calmly, as I take a moment to breath, and responds, "All of the above!" She remains silent for a few seconds, then adds that it took her a long time to get there and explains it all started with engaging in internal work.

"I took over the responsibility of leading the climate negotiations six months after the Copenhagen disaster. At my very first press conference in that role, I was asked by a journalist, 'Ms. Figueres, do you think a global agreement will ever be possible?', and I answered, 'Not in my lifetime'. As I heard myself saying it, I felt horrified, frozen. I thought, 'Wait a minute, those words went straight out of my mouth, without passing through my brain, and certainly not through my heart'. And I started thinking, 'What would be the consequence if what I just said turns out to be true?' and I saw all my nightmares about social justice become a reality. That's when I decided that 'not having an agreement in my lifetime simply cannot happen'. And I remember so well exiting that conference room, walking to my office, knowing all of a sudden what my mission was going to be: change the global mood on climate change. That one simple question and my pessimistic answer started me on a path, the path to prove my own prediction wrong. I didn't know at that time that it would result in a global agreement. I just knew that I was going to have to change the predominant pessimistic mindset on climate change. And I also knew that it had to start with me, since I was the first one to project that despondency. If I was living that paralysis in my own mindset, that pessimism, then I had absolutely no right or moral standing to ask anyone else to change. So that's what I did: a lot of work on myself, to change just that. Now I can tell you how to do it, but I didn't know it back then, and, of course, such a change doesn't happen in a couple of days. It took time and effort to figure out how to change my sense of catastrophe, how to open up, to go through an internal arc of transformation, that took me into the space of possibility. Not even a space of delivery of the agreement, just a space of possibility. But I had to figure it out for myself, and only then would I have been ready to take the next step—which was to change the attitude of my team".

Christiana asks to borrow my pen. She draws four circles on a piece of paper in front of us.

"If you think about systems and processes, you can conceive a series of concentric circles. I was at the core, so first I had to work on Christiana. The next concentric circle was my team, those 500 people who worked at the Secretariat of the UNFCCC and who were also completely despondent because they were largely blamed for the disaster in Copenhagen. Working with my team became my second priority, to evoke that arc of transformation for them. And we managed to build them up, slowly but surely, from a dysfunctional and despondent team to the top performing team of the United Nations, which they were by 2015", she says while pointing to the second concentric circle with the pen.

She moves the pen slightly and continues, "The next concentric circle was, of course, the governments of the world. They are the major 'clients' of the climate change convention. Of course, you get the gist by now", she says laughing. "They were also completely despondent. Many of them were not even willing to talk to each other because they had gone through such a painful experience in Copenhagen. So we had to begin to shine a light and then have that light that starts at the centre move out to these concentric circles. It was a process that took several years. But it worked also because of another element: we built a fourth and final circle, which was not there before these years—we were very explicit in reaching out to many stakeholders who had been held at bay by the system. You know how the system works?", she asks me.

I nod and respond that from my experience it invites civil society, youth, women, scientists, to say they were present, to tick the box, rather than to listen to them.

"Exactly", Christiana confirms. "We did the opposite. We pulled them in, in a constructive manner, to build what we ended up calling a *surround sound system* for the governments. Whether governments turned to young people, to religious and spiritual communities, to technology providers, to scientists, to old people, to nurses, to doctors, to women's groups, to the finance sector . . . in whichever direction they turned, they would get the same message: 'we want an agreement, and it has to be an ambitious one'".

Christiana starts drawing arrows across the circles. "It was an iterative process, across all of those concentric circles. And, if you understand how complex adaptive systems work, which obviously this one is, then you understand that whatever happens at one level of the system actually happens in a very similar fashion at all other levels of the system. And this is how you can bring about change: if you get stuck at one level, let's say the government level, you can go to another level of the system and move a piece and that helps unlock the level at which you are stuck. It was the understanding of complex adaptive systems that helped to smoothen out the way, that moved us from being in an 'impossible' situation to a 'maybe', then a 'perhaps', then 'likely under certain conditions', then 'possible', and finally to a 'delivered' agreement. It was an arc that brought us to this historical agreement . . ."

"Imagine", she adds, putting down the pen, "how a simple question from a journalist and my pessimistic answer started me on this path, to change what I had just said. I'm still looking for that journalist to thank him for it—it turned my thinking around".

OVERCOMING DESPONDENCY, AFFIRMING OPTIMISM

In today's society, despondent thinking on climate change is common currency. According to a 2021 study conducted by Lancet across 10 countries, children and young people (aged 16 to 25) suffer from anxiousness, sadness, anger, helplessness, powerlessness, and guilt because of climate change. A total of 45% of the respondents said these feelings negatively impact their daily lives and functioning. Overall, 59% of them were extremely worried about climate change, and 84% reported being at least moderately worried. These young people feel more betrayed than reassured by governmental action trying to address climate change. We see this outrage in the eyes of the millions of girls and boys taking to the streets, of scientists and experts trying to ring the alarm bell despite often remaining unheard, of the few politicians trying to push ambitious climate action amid pushbacks by colleagues or lobbyists. Like many of you, I also feel outraged at how long it's taking governments, corporates to act seriously and collectively on climate change. But we can't stop at outrage: our world needs us to denounce *and* to act, to feel upset *and* hopeful. Because our planet requires change and, only by holding outrage and optimism together, we stand a chance of delivering it. So, I ask Christiana, the queen of outrage and optimism, what advice she has for the outraged and the optimists of this world.

"Before going on to advice, I just want to warn that optimism is not naivete, right? It doesn't mean that we don't understand the science; it doesn't mean that we assume somebody else is going to fix it for us; it doesn't mean that we don't understand the urgency. There's none of that naivete or lack of information in being an optimist. The way I define *optimism* is that it is a very necessary input to any challenge. It's not the result of success, which I call a celebration, but it's an input—it goes in at the beginning of the process. And it is a choice. I wake up every morning and read very bad news, about climate or social injustice—we all know bad news travels fastest. And it's very difficult when faced with it to lift up your head and say to yourself, 'I'm going to do something about this'. It's easier to give up. That's why it's a choice. So to those of us who look at the world from a glass half full—I assume you are one of us, right?" she asks as I smile back, nodding. "I want to ask you to continue doing just that. We need your energy, your capacity to lift up your head, to lift others up, and do something to halt climate change", Christiana says in an encouraging tone.

She takes a few seconds to reflect. In a calmer, maternal voice, she adds, "And to those who don't have that muscle yet, the muscle of optimism: think of it as the same choice you have for your physical health. You choose what to eat, whether to exercise. And if you've never run in your life, you don't start with a marathon the next day, right? You start by walking—five minutes, ten minutes. The same thing applies to optimism, to action. The way you build up your physical health is similar to the way you go about building your mental health. Of course, there's always the choice of not building your mental health and of allowing all the bad news, the fear, to overtake and paralyse us. That is obviously a choice. Just like with physical health, you can choose to be sick, to continue feeling unhealthy. Or you can do something about it. So, it's a choice, your choice. It's as simple as that. It doesn't mean that you go from feeling fear and despair about climate change to being thrilled and effecting a vast change in global policy in 24 hours. But you can start with little things. And little things become bigger and bigger".

Christiana picks up the pen again to write down "action". She stares at the word, and adds, "Literature shows that the only way to move from doomerism on climate change to any degree of hope and light passes through the portal of action. Meaning you can't think your way out of it, because our mind will bring us back constantly and recurrently to the bad news we are exposed to. But you can act your way out of it. You can break the mould of what our mind tells us, by doing something that is positive . . . Believe me, it works—I tried it on my own skin. And that positive act begins to open up the possibility of a different mindset, of a different behaviour. This is the work I had to do on myself, with my teams, with global governments, which opened the way to the Paris Climate Agreement".

I think doing this work is what leadership is all about. And to get there, it takes a lot of courage, perseverance, and strength.

"Now, *post facto*, I recognise there was leadership there", admits Christiana, "but it was never intended as such. It was much more of a ground up thing, of a commitment to affect necessary change, rather than a need to lead. And yes, to get there it took strength—but not the typical definition of 'strength'. I see it more as an honesty, a self-awareness, that is ironically grounded in vulnerability. It takes being willing to dig into where we feel comfortable and uncomfortable, into what we know and don't know, what makes us laugh and what makes us cry. In my case, by now, I don't even need to dig into my vulnerability: it sort of erupts . . . I've been publicly known to burst into tears, because my passion and my vulnerability are simply a part of me, which I don't have to hide in order to give a strong image to the outside. Honestly", she says as her eyes get teary, "show me a person, a human who's not vulnerable. Show me a human who hasn't suffered and who continues to not suffer. We are all humans, all struggling to do our best, and I know that in each of us there is a soft side. And through that soft side, our humanity, we can reach each other, we can find the common ground we are losing more of, every single day".

STRONG BACK, SOFT FRONT

Christiana shares that she went through a spiritual journey in her life. As a result of her unexpected divorce which left her feeling lost, lonely, and depressed, she found the teachings of Thich Nhat Than, a Zen Buddhist master, who helped her reconnect with herself and face difficult moments. She did so right in the midst of leading international climate negotiations, as part of her personal arc of transformation.

One of her other teachers is Roshi Joan Halifax, an American Buddhist teacher, an ecologist, a civil rights activist, and an anthropologist. And Christiana tells me that Joan has a beautiful way of explaining this articulation between strength and vulnerability.

"I am only now beginning to understand what Roshi Joan has been saying for years, how these two elements coexist. And I want to share her framework because it helped me, and I hope it can help others understand it as well: she calls it the combination of a soft front and a strong back. The *strong back* is the part that holds us firmly grounded in our values, in our principles, it's the lighting and guiding star in our life. But life is not a highway, a straight line from A to B. Life is much more of a meandering river. And there are many rocks in the river, and it has many turns. So yes, of course, we all have a guiding light. But we also must develop flexibility if we want to get from A to B. And that flexibility is what Roshi Joan calls the *soft front*. This flexibility starts by understanding that we, that I, am vulnerable and will always be vulnerable—despite all the internal work I can do on myself. All of us are, with our moments of doubt, fear, anxiety, and that's fine. And that's fine", repeats Christiana, as if saying that to herself. Then she looks at me and continues, "That's where we can touch each other. That's where we learn from ourselves and from others. And leadership to me is that: alternating our strong back with our soft front, or even better, learning how to make them coexist to generate change. It's not the machete-like leadership we see, but a nuanced exercise of bringing change within ourselves and within our world".

As soon as I hear these words, this explanation of a strong back and a soft front, I feel somehow relieved. In my own career, in my own life, I often felt as if I needed to choose between projecting one or the other element: the strong, grounded, purpose-driven part, or the flexible, vulnerable, human part.

I felt that in the mainstream definition of "leadership", or more simply of "management", people expected me to be strong, grounded, sure of the choices I make for myself, for the team, for the organisations I lead. Though I also felt that if you are too strong or confident, you risk being perceived as stiff, unrelatable, single-minded—especially if you're a woman. At the same time, showing vulnerability, doubt, too much flexibility, can also be quickly interpreted as weakness, which, in turn, can feed your insecurities. Finding your way, the virtuous balance between the soft and the strong amid societal pressure is tough work. But this framework suddenly helps me define the complementarity of these two skills, attitudes, ways of being, which are naturally part of me, of us, even when we feel unsure about how to express them. Roshi Joan's words give me within a few seconds the confidence that by combining them, not by choosing between them, we can accelerate change, make the right choices, lead from a space of humanity—holding together the strength and the softness.

I share this thought with Christiana, and she gets a big smile on her face. "You know", she tells me as she leans in towards me, "if I had to give one piece of advice to my younger self, it would be exactly around this. About getting in touch with my soft part earlier than I did in my lifetime. For many women, what is difficult to access is the strong path. I didn't have issues with that, maybe because I grew up in a patriarchal system and house in which that was a dominant trait. To me, the soft front was the difficult one to access, and I only accessed it because life gave me huge, huge suffering and difficulties I had to live through. And that's where all of that emerged, was evoked. If I had to do it all over again, I would tell myself to access both, in equal measures. To not be afraid of that part that gets me in touch with my vulnerability, my fear, my sense of insufficiency, my self-doubt. So many of us run away from it because we don't know what to do with it. While what we must do is the opposite: open space for it, allowing that part to come forward, to deal with it in a loving and calm way. Because if you run away from it, it controls your life, but if you welcome it and interlace it into your thinking, feeling, actions in a way that is constructive and positive, then it nurtures your life. And I'll tell you something else", she quickly touches my hand as a sign of closeness, "the magic of it all is to find how that soft part allows you to be more grounded, more present, less volatile. It is not a matter of control but a matter of resilience. It's the difference between the tree that gets toppled by the storm and the bamboo that manages to bend with the storm. I want to be a bamboo tree that bends with the storm and comes back up stronger than before. Because that gives me so much more resilience, as well as empathy for all of those who are also in a storm. I wish I had figured that out earlier, so I am happy to hear this framework might help you—and hopefully those reading my words—do just that".

PLANTING FORWARD

Women are often constrained and held back by stereotypes and external judgements. If you are confident, you are bossy. If you are empathic, you are weak. If you are a stay-at-home mum, you are not fulfilling your feminist-career agenda, and if you are a working mum, you are constantly pulling a too- short blanket between work and home and feeling you're failing at both, and then if you are not a mum, you failed to fulfil your reproductive societal role . . . and it goes on and on. Whatever you do, someone will be there ready to deem it wrong—as it has been happening for centuries. And this of course generates a distorted self-image of ourselves as women.

"Our countries are full of structural inequalities, barriers, glass ceilings—there is no question about that", says Christiana responding to my train of thoughts on stereotypes. "But if only we understood better who we are and if only we had more confidence in ourselves, as women, then we would become much more effective in changing structural inequalities and in claiming the positions we deserve. It is not our fault: we swallowed for too long the wrong pill, the pill of inferiority, the pill of patriarchy. But we have the power to change this. By changing our self-perception, our self-image. By starting to swallow the right pill and making sure we give this pill to our daughters—be it through education, through parenting, through role models. This is the only way to break the cycle we are stuck in—by planting forward, starting from changing women's and girls' self-image".

I note down on my sheet of questions the expression "planting forward", as it sounds much nicer than giving back, which is what I commonly use. Christiana notices me writing it down and explains that planting forward comprises many different steps: "it takes fertilising the ground, then planting the seeds, then watering the seeds. Every process we are in, in our personal or professional life, is at one of these stages. Sometimes, the ground we find is fertile, and you can put the seeds in. Sometimes you already find the seeds, and you think, 'Alright, let's pass to the watering stage'. So you must figure out at what stage of this cycle you are at, but you must also understand that these stages are all necessary and are iterative. It doesn't mean that if you water and it blooms you don't have to start back and fertilise at some point—the important thing though is to continue planting and planting forward".

As Christiana speaks, I feel the power and the optimism embedded in the decision to invest our energy in fixing the future rather than on looking backwards.

"My north star of social justice is very much future oriented because I can't change what has gone wrong before me: decisions, investments, policies, injustices made before my time", explains Christiana. "But I can focus on the present and on the future, by planting forward. I want women, human beings, animals, nature to have a better world, after me. This is as basic as the terms of reference (ToR) of being a mother. I understand not all women have decided to or can be mothers, and I respect that. But for me the ToR of a mother are to create conditions that are conducive and enable greater well-being for those who follow you. My work on climate change, or on opening up the path for more women to participate at all levels of our society, is all about being a mother—it's just an extension of that. I do it for my daughters, and I do it for all the women surrounding me, and the ones yet to come . . . or at least I try".

Literature recognises the existence of feminine traits, and some think they are linked to our biological reproductive capacity. We start listing some of them together: inclusion, greater capacity to combine long-term and short-term thinking and actions, more sincere and authentic communication, a greater willing-ness to meet across the table, and empathy—allowing us to see more easily the human part within each and every one of us.

"Those traits are considered feminine maybe because the average woman expresses them and lives them more deeply and more explicitly than the average man, which doesn't mean men don't have them or can't express them as well", says Christiana,

adding a nuance to the mainstream perspective. "It's very difficult to say with confidence what is a feminine trait and what is
not. But there is one thing I can say confidently: these traits are
sorely missing out there. I would want to see men and women
bringing them to the decision-making tables way more often
than we currently do".

This is why Christiana, while heading the UNFCCC, worked
on creating structural changes: to open space for more women
within the UN and state diplomacy systems. By doing so, she
hoped to see more of these traits around decision-making tables.
"I saw very evidently during my time at the UN that there was
an increasing number of women coming into the negotiations—
whether that was through government teams, through young
activists, or any of the other channels of people entering the
system. Despite this, when I sat up there, on the podium, as
the head of the UNFCCC, I would look out and find a sea
of people and would be reminded of how atrociously obvious
it was that there wasn't equal representation of women and
that the decisions taken in that body were not gender-sensitive.
It became clear that something had to be done structurally to
accelerate gender equality and make it systemic. I worked with
amazing women to ensure the COP called on the participation
of more women in its various bodies and that we have gender-
sensitive measures and metrics across the legal documents of
the Convention".

Christiana's expression changes—she is thinking back to those
times, as if she is reminded of something else. "I do remember
one time, when we had just finished working through all of
this: creating a women's programme, adding quotas, passing a
decision on women's participation. I was so proud, along with
many other people inside and outside the secretariat who had

worked hard to advance women's empowerment. Until the moment one negotiator from a European country came up to me and said, 'Christiana, I thought you were sensitive to women's issues'. I replied, 'Yes, I thought so too', and she said, 'You are not'. I was baffled, but managed to say 'OK, show me'. This negotiator looked straight into my eyes, and explained: 'I am here, I have been negotiating for two weeks, all day and night. And I have a newborn baby, and no place to breast feed'. I felt I had just been slapped in the face. Because here we were, doing all of that, the legal statements, the macro decisions, but clearly not doing enough at the micro level. This was an amazing lesson for me, that I share here because it's a lesson for us all: it's not about changing only the macro level; you also must change the micro, which is the level that allows more people to participate. We had thought about so many other things, but none of us had thought about something as basic as the fact that we might have incredibly courageous negotiators or staff who have joined us in the first few months after the birth of their child. People like me who work on the planetary level tend to forget that it's not only about that level: it must trickle all the way down, to daily habits of people, to where it really makes a difference. In about three seconds, we repurposed a room for breastfeeding of course", she says with a cheeky smile—while I imagine her running around and moving furniture to make it happen, "but I'll never forget this lesson".

FEMALE LEADERS VERSUS FEMINIST LEADERS

Speaking of empowering women, at the macro and micro level, I share with Christiana that I have been recently struggling with a leader in my home country. Italy, after centuries of male emperors, kings, and, more recently, presidents and prime ministers, has elected its first-ever woman prime minister—Giorgia Meloni.

A historical step for our country, no doubt about that. What I struggle with is that, at least from my point of view, Meloni doesn't see herself as a woman who should lift other women or minorities up—despite having lived the discrimination in her own skin. She rather sees herself as a woman who can and wants to play by the existing patriarchal rules of the game—and this self-perception is translated into policies which are restricting the rights of the LGBTQI+ community in Italy, of migrants, and which are focused on promoting the role of women as mothers. This self-perception is best shown by Meloni's symbolic choice to not be called *la presidente*, with the feminine article, but *il presidente*—with the masculine article. Our first woman prime minister is referred to with the masculine pronouns, because power—in her view—is masculine. But it's not that easy. I struggle, in parallel, also with this idea that any woman reaching a top leadership position is expected to lift everybody up. An expectation, a burden, which is not put on men, but is always put on women. And I can't reconcile these competing feelings within me.

"Well", reacts Christiana while writing down *burden* on the piece of paper, "I have that expectation of lifting others up and fixing the world both for men and for women leaders. And from my perspective, as a world leader, I never saw it as a burden, but as an opportunity for yet more change. Opening up possibilities for women serves so many other purposes: it serves the human rights purpose—women have the right to participate shoulder to shoulder; it also is very helpful for having better decisions around the table—so even if you are very utilitarian and you think you need better policy decisions, then it's in your interest to get women around the table, to make sure you have diversity of thought and reach better decisions; it also helps with climate change policy, because when you have women on board, they will think about things that maybe men typically wouldn't think of—coming back to my example of the nursing room. Of course, it does take a village and the burden cannot be put on one person—be it a woman or a man—but we must expect leaders to play a role in correcting the legacy we have all received. A legacy of thousands of years in which boys and men were given more educational, professional opportunities, which has led to decisions in technology, health, education, finance, that are privileging men over women, to policies and investments which are blind to gender parity. This is what it is", she notes down *blind*. "People are sometimes blind to their blindness. And maybe this is what happens to certain women in leadership positions, like you were saying. They are so blinded by the patriarchal system that they don't understand they are not seeing their own blindness. To use the previous example of a strong back and soft front, I bet these are often women who have strong backs but have not cultivated the soft front. And that's a shame because by not cultivating the soft front, they curtail the possibility of accepting and driving change—not only for themselves but for humanity as a whole".

Christiana reminds me that she knows a thing or two about growing up in a patriarchal household. "I grew up in a male-dominated family, society, country. There was no doubt that my dad was the largest figure within our house and beyond, he was calling the shots. Imagine that", she says while leaning back in her chair, "I remember sitting at the dinner table and my mum saying, 'Children, don't speak, because your father is thinking'". She becomes quiet, sitting with that last sentence as if trying to digest it. "No wonder my three brothers grew up feeling part of this patriarchal structure. And on my side, it also seemed totally normal, part of life. I didn't think I should rebel to this—I just found my space and adopted the strong back, imitating the men and the women in my family. And to be honest, it is only since I started following my own spiritual path that I realised I could do all of that male thing very well but that I was missing out on 50% of who I am, the feminine side of me. It wasn't society that taught me how to connect to it, it was my personal spiritual path—after a painful divorce and family losses—that helped me do just that. And once I did it, I realised that that 50% was the key to get me to where I wanted to go—professionally and personally".

"I am very grateful for having discovered that because now of the three brothers, I have lost 2". As she says these words, Christiana gets tears in her eyes. She shares that as we sit in this meeting room in London, she is losing yet another sibling on the other side of the ocean. I take her hand, as tears stream down her face. I get teary as well as I witness her pain, unsure of how I can be of help. With a broken voice, Christiana decides to continue.

"It is very clear to me that I have moved into the role of the matriarch of the family. Probably the first matriarch in I don't know how many generations. This means that the reference point of the family has shifted for the first time to the female part of the family. As unfortunate as it is given the circumstances, it is a very interesting shift. My nieces and nephews aren't even aware of the fact that in the previous generation it was all about the men. And they find no problem with the fact that now it is many of us women that hold the power—myself, my sisters, my daughters. The most beautiful thing is that we are leading from a very soft front and a very tough back. We are managing to bring that balance that we didn't have in previous generations, and this makes me so proud of the women in my family. You know, my daughters, who are in their early 30s, were just born with that chip—with that balance. I remember one night, I was sitting next to their bed saying their nightly prayer—as they were still children, and when I said, 'Amen', one of them said, 'Mum, it's not AMEN, it's a AWOMEN'"—Christiana starts laughing as she dries her tears.

LA PAZ SIN FIN

"You remember the name of my father's farm?", I say *La Lucha Sin Fin*. "Good. Now that I have lived my years and that I also have a home, I decided to name it *La Paz Sin Fin* [Peace without End]. Because I think we need both: to constantly find the next frontline of challenges and go at it with everything that we have but—if we want to have that positive impact—we must also exercise our degree of self-care, find that serenity and peace within us. Otherwise, we will go out there with a fire torch and set fire to everything—sometimes, that's necessary but mostly it is not, and we risk to only do damage. My motto is to balance the struggle with the equanimity, the outrage with the optimism: they are the yin and yang, they belong together, they are indivisible. Of course, you can't reach that balance every single day, at least I don't", she adds with a big honest smile, "but I aspire to it, and that helps me get where I want to go".

While hearing Christiana's stories, about her family, her struggles, her accomplishments, her growth as a woman, a friend, a mother, and a leader, I tell myself she has already contributed so much to society that she would easily deserve to drop the mic and enjoy life in her *Paz Sin Fin* home for many years to come. But I am reminded of the struggle without end, the other half of her, and want to know what is coming next—as I know she is far from being done with the change she wants to see.

"Well, as I have learned over the past two years, you never know how long your lifetime is. I have started thinking of myself as being 66 years closer to death . . . We treat death as a taboo topic, but we are all walking in that direction". I perceive a sombreness to her voice which I had not heard so far. "This is why I don't want to speak of what I want to see in my lifetime, but what I would like to see happen, independent of whether I am here or not". She stops speaking, and tears start to fall again from her big dark eyes. Her voice is broken, but she powers through: "First and foremost, I want to see less inequality. The inequality that we are witnessing is just deeply painful to me—be it of gender, income, sexual preference . . . I can't believe our world is still this inequal, and I can't tolerate not seeing this change". As her voice cracks further and tears continue to fall, she asks a simple question, "Can human society evolve to a higher level of consciousness and awareness? A level which would allow us to see each other as human beings, all of whom have the same rights and the same access to well-being?"

She remains silent for a few seconds as we both realise how hard the answer to such a simple question is. She wipes her tears and goes on, "I would also like to see the damage that we are making to the natural world decreased and reversed. Can we stop deforestation and move into reforestation and regeneration? Can we stop the biodiversity loss and give back room to nature? And my third question is: can we see that we are all inter-related? Because if we regenerate ourselves, if we understand who we are, then we will understand that all life on this planet is inter-related, that we all depend on each other. It is not a situation in which human beings are a superior species and everything else is inferior to us . . . that is such a fallacy!"

As she was speaking, Christiana drew three circles with a question mark in the centre of each, on a little corner of this—by now—full piece of paper. Pointing to these circles, she concludes, "We must bring the human species to a higher level of conscious-ness and action, to understand that all things are deeply inter-related, and by doing so to regenerate nature. I don't know how long I will live, if it's one day, one month, or 20 years, but to me those three would be worth fighting for and fixing within the twenty-first century".

Christiana still has teary eyes, as her alarm clock goes off. "Oh, it's time to run to my board meeting", she says. I stop the recording and start packing—Christiana is already up and ready to go, but instead of leaving she starts helping me pack. We walk out of the business centre together, and leave with a hug, thanking each other for the conversation we just had.

Outside it's raining—a typical grey day in London. I feel ener-getic, inspired, touched by this meeting with Christiana, which makes rainy London look nostalgic, somehow romantic. I pull out my umbrella and make my way to the co-working space. As I pull out my computer to catch up on emails from the past few hours, a paper falls out of my backpack. It's Christiana's notes, which I took by mistake along with the printed ques-tions for the interview. A paper which captures the essence of this interview. The concentric circles of change, which starts with each and every one of us at its core. The values and words that define Christiana's philosophy of life and of leadership: vulnerability, change, outrage, optimism. And, finally, the three question marks, with which she leaves us all. Wondering what my role, your role will be in helping humanity find answers, by using our outrage and our optimism to lead the change our world so urgently needs.

• 2 •

CURIOSITY
Gitanjali Rao

"HI, I AM GITANJALI". I hear a voice coming from the screen, look up and see Gitanjali smiling as she has just joined our video call. She is sitting in her bedroom in Denver, the US, and I am sitting in mine in Italy. This distance somehow makes me nervous: I love seeing people in person, observing their body language, chit-chatting, and connecting beyond screens, especially for this type of an interview. I smile back, respond, "Hi, I am Gaia" and straight away try to catch some elements from what surrounds her—maybe to make the distance disappear. A poster of old airplanes, a college flag, and a copy of a van Gogh painting. This takes us up to 7 seconds, the fatidic time to gather a first impression of a person—according to a Princeton study—which seems positive: smiling into our screens, the distance feels already gone.

It's Sunday, January 2023, and by the time I join the call, it's already getting dark outside. I have just come home after a long hike—during which I checked several times that I had got the nine-hour time difference right—combed my hair, changed out of my sports clothes, and sat down for the interview.

"I literally woke up 20 minutes ago": it's 8:30 AM for Gitanjali and I tell myself that nothing would have gotten my 17-year-old self out of bed before 10 AM on a Sunday morning. But she is fully switched on and ready for the day, "I have a busy day ahead. This interview and then my flying course"—as if going to a pilot training is the most natural Sunday activity.

"Next week I have the exam for my licence. I have been training for this for years, meaning that today is not a class like all the others, it's *the* class before the exam". We start chatting about flying and how it gives us a whole new perspective on the world,

on how tiny we are as human beings. My only flying experiences were that of a parachute jump over the Wadi Rum desert
in Jordan and paragliding a couple of times in the Alps, just to
get that feeling, that adrenaline rush and perspective. Gitanjali
explains to me that her dad is a private pilot and as a kid she
always knew that once she turns 13, she would take lessons
and learn how to fly a plane. And this is what she did—the first
testament of her determination and unconventional character.

But flying is not the only thing Gitanjali has had clear ideas
about since a very young age. "I was four when my uncle gave
me a chemistry kit. Okay, I did ask for a Barbie dream house,
like a normal four-year-old, but as soon as I had that kit in
my hands, I couldn't stop. I spent hours exploring the world,
running experiments, learning how things worked. And I've
practically never stopped since".

Gitanjali has by now come up with over 10 innovations,
of which three are at the prototype stage and one has been
released. Her innovations respond to deeply different sets of
problems: lead-contaminated water, snake bites, cyber bullying, opium addiction.

"Over the years, I have been coming up with my own ideas, my
own inventions, my unique ways of tackling problems to which I
felt I had a personal connection. Problems I heard about on TV,
from my family or my friends. I didn't want to sit here and wait
for someone else to come up with a solution—I wanted to find
that solution myself". Her voice is warm, kind and determined.
"That's how I was brought up: 'if you don't like something, fix it
yourself'. And that's how I felt: I was not content with the state
of the world, with all the problems I was seeing and no one doing
anything about them. So I took the first steps as a five-year-old,

as an eight-year-old, and then as an 11-year-old—I read books, online resources, MIT reviews, and even expert research reports, to come up with ideas and fix things. Ideas which maybe no one could use at that stage but that hopefully somebody will be able to use at some point in the future".

All these ideas and inventions brought Gitanjali to where she is today: a 17-year-old who is the first-ever Kid of the Year to feature on the cover of *TIME* magazine, who has an unmatched passion for science, several other recognitions on her CV, and a big choice to make in the coming few months: "I applied for several colleges here in the US that match my interests and provide research opportunities: to MIT, Harvard, Yale, Duke, Princeton, and Stanford. And by this spring, I need to choose where I want to go—right now I am evaluating these options every day, to figure out the right match for me".

CARVING HER PATH

Gitanjali is clearly on the route to excellence within her field, Science, Technology, Engineering and Mathematics (STEM), and beyond. And she has been since she was a small kid. She has an incredibly clear idea of what she is passionate about, science and innovation, and of how she wants to pursue her passion.

"It's important to me for people to understand that this purpose, this drive, was never linked to one enlightening moment when I put all the pieces together. Rather this clarity came more naturally and gradually: I followed my instinct, and over time, that gave me an idea of what I love to do". I ask her what the magic formula is behind such a childhood and such a path—we laugh about the many times her parents were asked this exact same question. "Apart from a lot of good food", she adds with a smile, "I grew up in a household where curiosity was always enabled. I was never forced down a path but was rather exposed every day to the world around me. 'You name it, I did it', I was that kind of kid. I did ice-skating, played the piano, football, I took cooking classes, magic classes, Irish step dancing, pottery . . . I did the weirdest things, using the local recreation centre and summer camps—inexpensive options to explore the world. Some of them obviously didn't stick—like football was absolutely not for me—but others did: I still fence today, play the piano, and am working on getting my pilot licence. I remember my parents repeating to me over and over again that they would give me the opportunity to try things and take risks, to look at the world, but that I would have to carve my own path. By having this liberty to carve my own path, no matter the age, I started exploring my passion for science and it took me where I am today", she says with a sparkle in her eyes. "The biggest piece of advice I would give parents, as a kid, as a girl in STEM, is to not undermine the value of exposure, especially at an extremely young age. Because it is so incredibly important that every kid out there gets the same chance I got: to explore the world and forge their own path. There is literally no point in forcing a kid down a predetermined road, because it gets them nowhere. On the contrary, if they find their passion, that drive will get them everywhere".

I try to hint at the fact that objectively speaking, she is a particularly smart girl and that me—and most of the kids I knew—were not inventing things at the age of five or six.

"I am always told that I am smart, or people ask my mum what she put in my food to make me become who I am", she says laughing. "But what I really am is super hard-working, and everyone can be hard-working, as long as they find what they are passionate about. So take those risks at a young age, or allow your kids to take those risks, and do whatever comes to you next. If there is an opportunity knocking on your door, take it and learn through it, no matter how young or old you are!", she says in a passionate voice.

Gitanjali likes speaking of Ikigai, the Japanese concept which means "a reason for being" (生き甲斐): what gives a person a sense of purpose. In her case, she found it in science, in innovation. She did so thanks to her parents' support in exploring the world, but not just that. "It takes a village to raise a child", I ask her to try and unpack for me what this village looks like in her case. School, role models, mentors, friends, each of them have an immense impact in shaping our life trajectory, especially for children and teenagers.

"I am lucky, I found people, mentors, ready to invest their time in me. It's thanks to them that I developed my skill set, that I learned new things: by being given the space and the trust of trying, failing, getting back on my feet, and doing it all over again. That's how I grew into an innovator—I learned what I know about the bioengineering field and that's how I now find myself talking to you and sharing my story. My mentors are the people I work with in labs, the ones who take the time to listen to my ideas, let me shadow them for weeks at a time, and make an effort to ensure I learn and gain experience. They do so today, but what is even more surprising is that they did so when I was 11 or 12", she pauses for a few seconds to find the right words, then carries on. "Taking that chance on a 12-year-old who has little more than a dream in her head is such an uncommon thing to do, but it changed my life. Still, the reality today is that very few people would say 'let's allow a child into the lab and see what they can do'. But those are the experiences that change a child's life, that allow a child to explore, learn, and emerge, and this is why we need more and more professionals ready to take that chance", she adds, fervently.

"I also found mentors within my school—my physics teacher was the most important one to me. He was that one person who never had expectations—in the best possible way. His everyday goal was to get children to learn: his was the hardest class at school but he made it seem as the easiest A—because it was principally about learning, about giving students the space to experiment, not about grading. That's the sort of environment I wish every student would get encouraged in: one where adults are willing to let them learn, to tell them to take risks and opportunities, to mentor them, not to scare them with grades that often don't reflect your actual learning. Kids are curious, and we must let them use their curiosity to explore and learn about the world, and by doing so, I am sure we'll get way more Gitanjali's in this world: ready to use what they learn to solve problems, not to only get good grades".

IT STARTS AT SCHOOL, AND IT STARTS WITH KINDNESS

This support system in and out of school is not what all children get though. This is why quality schooling is so fundamental: the educational system is what can give each child the same opportunity, no matter the family background, their socioeconomic status, their gender or the colour of their skin, and what can allow any child to thrive and maybe one day emerge as a leader.

"Or at least that's how it should be", Gitanjali tells me eagerly, showing she wants to dig into this topic further. "For this to happen, we need to fix many things within our schools. Starting with the diversity of mentors and role models: of teachers, of staff members, of historical figures we study or read about. Seeing people that look just like you sends such an empowering message", her tone becomes hopeful. "I actually didn't know until I was six or seven that I *could* be a scientist. I discovered it wasn't a job exclusively for men the moment I first heard about Marie Curie. Since then, she has been my role model".

We know indeed that by age six children start classifying jobs along gender lines: how many times have we seen in schoolbooks that the girl is the mum, the princess or the nurse, and the boy is everything else? So, no wonder that by age 12, 50% of girls already aspire to take up gender-stereotyped roles, with huge implications on the decisions they make about their future studies and career direction.

"Finding women who I could look up to, who had something in common with me, was a crucial discovery. They helped me figure out that anyone can pursue the job they want, which meant I could aspire to be a scientist, despite being a South Asian–looking girl". We continue discussing systemic change and lack of diversity within schools—Gitanjali shares a surprisingly understanding perspective: "I don't think this lack of diversity is something we are doing on purpose. It's due to unconscious biases: all of us are passing on traditional stereotypes from one generation to another. But the fact that it's not done on purpose doesn't mean we shouldn't break the cycle we are in—we have to break it, by changing the traditional education system and adding diversity to it".

But Gitanjali's ideas on what needs to change within our schooling system don't stop at diversity. "School reform is something I could speak of all day, so please stop me if I go on for too long", she says laughing. She puts her hands together, which I take as a sign of excitement, and I tell her to take all the time she needs. "The foremost thing we should do is teach kids about technology rather than scare them off. I go to a STEM school, so I have more of an opportunity than other kids to learn just this—but for my friends who don't go to such schools, they don't learn about technology in the same way I do. We should bring all the tech we have on the school table, teaching it not as a class but as an experience, as a *learning-by-doing* thing, and this is true for all subjects. We deserve an education which allows us to fail and learn with hands-on problem-solving, rather than focusing on grades and lectures by teachers. And this innovative approach is even more important when it comes to technology: by now it is so deeply intertwined with our lives that we can't afford to have a generation of kids who don't understand it, learn how to use it, and know how to leverage it for good".

To make such a shift, schools need resources, competencies, and only a minority of privileged schools in the US or across the globe can afford to do this. "I am aware of this", responds Gitanjali. "This is why the next step is connecting more privileged schools, such as mine, with those in rural communities or in countries where children typically have less opportunities. We must use the resources of privileged areas to empower as many kids as we can, and the COVID-19 pandemic has taught us that there are no barriers to doing just this: connecting online, to put kids in touch from different schools and countries and to get teachers to exchange their insights and resources".

Gitanjali walks the talk: since a few years, she has been providing STEM workshops to students from all over the world—allowing kids from Mexico, India, and 40 other countries to attend classes and have a mutualistic learning experience. On the website, I read that the approach of these workshops involves a peer student-led session, hosted by Gitanjali, in which she shares her experience and tries to spread the spirit of innovation to solve world problems with her peers. "Innovation is not an option—it's a necessity. But I am very aware that one girl cannot solve all the world's problems, and that's why I want to mobilise other kids and teenagers like me to do the same", Gitanjali says with a proud look on her face. "I like to say that I am working towards the bigger goal of creating an innovation movement, a global community of young innovators that can play their part in solving world problems". A community which is growing at an incredible speed: since the launch of these workshops, Gitanjali has trained 70,000 students.

"That type of collaboration, across countries and cultures, is something I never thought I would see. Bringing it to light was an incredible experience: often, to be honest, I learn more from them than they learn from me", she adds, smiling.

What captivates me about Gitanjali is exactly this. It's not only her passion for STEM, for innovation, and her creativity in finding solutions to problems, but it's her kindness and her generosity in lifting others up.

"Kindness is my guiding principle", she states. "We need to involve kindness in all we do. Starting from school . . .", she cuts her sentence and says, "Sorry, I am still going on with the school part, is it OK?". I nod and smile and ask her to continue: "The last thing we must have in schools is to root everything in kindness. The reason we take classes is because we want to use what we learn to do something helpful for our world, for others. It's not to learn for the sake of learning. History without a purpose is just facts, mathematics without a purpose is just numbers. By now you must have figured it out, but I am the annoying kid who will stand up and say 'so what is the real purpose, the real-life application, of what we are learning?' And I am convinced it is a very valid question, especially for teenagers who are struggling to understand concepts and how they relate to their lives—and it's a question that more teachers should be asking themselves. And kindness can be the answer: how can we use what we are learning to help people or our planet? If we all keep that in mind, we could have a huge collective impact on our communities and on the world, even as kids".

This is what Gitanjali tries to do: innovate, rooting her work in kindness, and, by doing so, contribute towards fixing world problems. "To me, this should be the driving value for leaders: the capacity of understanding why we do what we do and what its impact is on our world and on others. Not money or company profit—but the impact and its added value to our common good . . . and sometimes, even with the best intentions, it will happen that we get things wrong or lose track of what should really guide us—it's part of life—but we must have the courage to admit when we do wrong, change, and adapt". She looks down and adds that the reality is very different: "We lost touch with this part of leadership, and it will take a massive effort to put kindness and the courage to learn back at its core".

LEADERSHIP IS NOT WHAT WE ARE TAUGHT, NOR WHAT WE SEE

We start talking about leadership, what it means to her, and if and how she would want this concept to evolve. Gitanjali shares that from her experience, one never has a single leader in one situation: "It always takes a village to make something happen. You just have more vocal people then that take credit for it!" We both laugh, and she continues speaking: "Leadership is an incredible trait, a trait that everybody is looking for: colleges, volunteering opportunities, youth movements. They all want leaders. I mean, they even teach it in high school through one-hour-long "leadership classes" . . . but the reality is that leadership is not what we are taught, what we write on our college application, or try to showcase when in public. Leadership is what YOU make out of all of this", she stops for a second, looks up, thinking, and then goes on. "It is not the YOU, it is the HOW—now that I come to think of it. HOW you conduct yourself with others, HOW you bring ideas to the table. I like to say that I am a leader *in the way* I run my workshops with other kids across the world, not *because* I am Gitanjali Rao".

There are thousands of definitions of leadership out there and—if you are reading this book—chances are you are also trying to figure out what it means to you. Gitanjali's twist from the YOU to the HOW is surely a good starting point. But it's just one part of it.

"Another side of it is that leadership should never benefit only you—it should always benefit the community". How many among the people we call "leaders" are actually trying to benefit the community, not only themselves? Some, for sure, but not enough. And the few that do are the ones who are remembered in history and looked back upon with admiration. If the common good, the added value to our communities, countries, planet, was the driver for leaders and the criteria by which we judge them, we wouldn't be where we are today: surrounded by ego wars and an unprecedented multiplicity of crises.

"I am worried about where the world stands today", says Gitanjali in a bitter voice. "What worries me the most is the contamination of natural resources, which is turning into a huge problem that too few people are talking about. One of my inventions is linked to this: I saw on TV kids like me drinking lead-contaminated water, with huge implications on their health, because of lack of better alternatives—of safe water—and of means to assess when water is not safe. And this is in the US, the richest country in the world!". Many cities in which we live, in the US and outside, have high levels of lead-contamination in water, due to old pipes, plumbing fixtures, and faucets. And most of us, indeed, are not aware of it—but data speaks loud: researchers indicate that in the US alone, nearly half of the population has been exposed to adverse lead levels in early childhood—impacting their health for the long-run. "My lead-detection portable device can hopefully help those people and kids know when water is not safe to drink and seek alternative water sources", continues Gitanjali, pragmatically—ready to move to her next point.

"The next thing that worries me is the unavailability of educational resources: they are incredibly important, but no one is investing in them. This is the case in the US but even more across the world. Quality education should be the cornerstone of our society and of our future, but *de facto* it's seen as an add-on, as something extra which is not a *must* have—leaving so many children behind". She quickly clears her voice and continues with a proud smile, "This is why I decided to run workshops with teenagers and kids from all over the world, but they are far from being enough . . . we need a systemic change for the problem to be fixed, not a 17-year-old running workshops. I don't see this change on the horizon though, which scares me", her smile is gone as she continues straight to the next point.

"The last thing that worries me is teenagers' mental health and digital mental health". Gitanjali shifts with complete ease from one topic to another, responding with her pragmatic approach to my question on world problems. I tell myself that I would need a one-day prep time to be able to articulate my top three concerns for humanity or our planet—let alone do something about it. "Mental health is a huge problem my generation is facing, but older people don't see it, which means nothing is being done about it".

I do a quick self-reflection, imagining that for Gitanjali I am part of "the older people" and tell myself that I have heard about it, that I know it has increased due to the COVID-19 lockdowns, but realise I don't have an idea of the size of the problem we are talking about. A quick google search and I find statistics from *Mental Health America* indicating that in the US, over 15% of boys and girls aged 12 to 17 have experienced a major depressive episode in 2022 alone—an increasing percentage over the past decade. I check data for Europe, as a true European at heart, and read in a UNICEF report that suicide is the second leading cause of death among young people aged 10 to 19—especially boys, who die by suicide at more than twice the rate of girls. "The situation is bad, and as young people, we must do something about it—as others are not. I am trying to contribute as I can: I created a service, Kindly, against cyberbullying. Kids can download it on their phones, or it can be invoked from different platforms, and it flags when we are using aggressive language—trying to stop bullying, one message at a time. A lot of us have been victims of or accomplices to bullyism, sometimes without even realising it, without knowing that what we do or say can hurt others, or that what others do to us can be classified as bullying". According to UNESCO, one-third of the globe's youth is bullied as of today. "But here again", continues Gitanjali, "we need a bigger focus, from schools, from parents, from doctors, from governments, from online platforms, to protect kids and support our mental well-being". She then goes on to explain that the service she created has been taken over by UNICEF's Office of Innovation, which is developing it as a digital public good to end cyberbullying and make children feel safer.

LOOKING UP

Speaking of her worries for today's world, I ask Gitanjali how it feels to look up to the generation of her parents, or grand-parents, as a 17-year-old with an acute awareness of the role these generations played in getting the world where it stands today, through unsustainable consumption and production models. While I ask the question I think of the pictures of pro-tests from youth movements, against pollution, fossil fuels, climate change. Of pictures of people her age, with so much rage in their eyes, who clearly feel adults have failed them, their generation, and the ones to come—and that they are continuing to fail them every single day, due to slow and inef-fective climate policies.

Gitanjali takes a moment to think, and then says something that surprises me. "Honestly, there are very mixed opinions on older generations. If you ask many climate activists, who have a lot of anger, they will say older generations ruined our environment. To an extent, that is a take on it and I can see where they come from. But I personally don't think that's how it is. I wouldn't be here, and my research wouldn't be here if not for the work that older generations did for years and years before me. I don't believe people like my parents or grandpar-ents, my teachers or mentors, purposefully created the climate crisis: it's simply that every day it's a new discovery, and back then, we were not aware of the consequences of our actions! In my view, nothing was done on purpose, nobody had a malicious intention—there are eight billion people too many for every person to have malicious intent", her look becomes less severe, she smiles and I take this statement as another example of how Gitanjali manages to put kindness above all.

"A starting point to shift this mentality of anger is understanding that it's not a one-person job, someone's specific role to fix the crises we are living in, while all the others wait on the sidelines, or protest against those few people. It's our collective responsibility, our collective passion for science and tech that can bring ideas and solutions to light. People from older generations can't work alone—they have the knowledge but often not the novelty of ideas, the thinking outside of the box. And it's the same for people in my generation—who have the novelty of youth ideas but not the skills to implement them in full. What we need to do right now, if we want to exit these multiple crises, is the opposite of what's happening. Put the rage aside, put the generational divide aside, and focus on fostering collaboration, using our respective strengths, to come up with cross-generational ideas that can fix our world".

Of course, this is the hard thing to do—and both Gitanjali and I acknowledge that. It's easier to complain and sit on the sidelines than to go and fix things, becoming one of the people who are observed and probably criticised by those on the sidelines. It's easier to show you are collaborating across generations while in reality—you are just ticking boxes, rather than doing the real hard work of holding inclusive discussions and carrying out decision-making processes. "I was at the UN General Assembly recently and the biggest theme was 'if you are a kid, pull a seat at the table, bring your insights to us'. It was great, I am a kid, a teenager by now, so I pulled the seat at the table. But I realised there is no point of pulling a seat at a table and sitting on it if no one pays attention to your insights: the perspective that kids bring is so much more important than what we think it is. I mean", she says while tying her hair up— with excitement in her eyes, "honestly, kids come up with the best ideas possible: they are creative, they have this blue-sky thinking that grown-ups don't have anymore, they are simply not as formatted. Kids contribute ideas which our world needs so desperately, but we need to be able to listen and foster such ideas—rather than say that a kid sat at the table and feel satisfied about that—that's far from being enough".

THE POWER OF DIVERSITY

That is true for youth, but it's true in many other contexts, including for women who are often given a seat at the table to tick the box rather than to have them fully occupy that seat.

"I can see that", says Gitanjali, "and I also lived this exclusion on my own skin as a young woman. But, before getting there, let me say something", she adds cheerfully. "Women bring so much to the table. I see it when I work with older women, but also among my girlfriends. Among everything they bring, the biggest thing is an intrinsic artistic sense—in anything they do. I know that sounds really stereotypical, but actually it's a proven fact that women and girls think and act in a more creative manner than men and boys. They bring a diverse way of doing things, new perspectives on ideas, including in tech and science, of which we need much more of. And this goes hand in hand with something else women typically bring to the table: a sense of multi-disciplinarity, a capacity to think and act across different fields—which, to say the least, has not been the strength of male scientists or innovators over the past decades. As women, we have this superpower of not getting stuck into one specific track but rather of opening new paths, new ways of combining ideas, creating different fields. And this is exactly what is needed to de-anchor traditional mechanisms and create a sense of novelty within the science and innovation fields. And yes, I am a woman, so this is very, very, biased, but I think it's true", she adds with conviction. "And I'll go even further: the perspective that women bring is so desperately needed, that we don't have a choice: our society will get to a point where it will understand that to maximise the level and quality of innovation, we need to bring in all the voices to the table and that having only middle-aged white men is not helping us out. We need the whole demographic if we want to fix world problems".

I see myself in the words of Gitanjali. My personal realisation, which increases every year, with every meeting, every new job, of the specificities I bring to the table as a woman manager, leader, as a female mentor to others—the same realisation that brought me to writing this book. And I see the power and the innovation that come with it—in a world built mainly by and for men. But I also see the stereotypes myself and so many other women have to navigate for us to be free to sit at the table and speak up—especially when we bring a different perspective than the dominant one.

"When it comes to stereotypes", says Gitanjali with a reassuring certainty in her voice, "part of it is realising that in the future, one day, there will be no stereotypes. There will be no such thing as 'girls in STEM', or 'youth in STEM', there will be only *people* in STEM. It is all going to mash eventually. I am convinced of that because society is only going up from here, from where we are today. We already see more diversity when it comes to the workforce. There are so many more opportunities than there were 50 years ago, for any of us to take up new things, to innovate across genders, across generations, or across countries. Maybe part of it is me being extremely optimist, which I am, but I really do think that we are looking at a future where there will be a truly diverse line-up when it comes to science and technology as well. And no, where we are now is by no means where we want it to be, but one day, we will reach that point—it's not an option not to—regardless of how long it takes. But until then, until the day of full inclusion, I like to tell girls what I tell myself: we might not be first in line, but we are *in* line—and that's more than what women could have said years ago. Take advantage of that opportunity, hold on to it, because you might not get another one again very easily. And, while doing so, be yourself—because that's your biggest superpower: it's being a woman, a girl of colour, a 17-year-old passionate about science and innovation. Eventually, people will want to hear from you, people will realise they need a different take on the world, and you'll be there ready to speak up and become first in line".

We start discussing what it takes for women—no matter the age—to become first in line. And the support system between women, as well as the allyship of men, is clearly on top in both of our minds. "There is a strong bond between men, a bond we need to see more of among women. And ideally between women and men. But I must also say that there is a very stereotypical perception of the white old male, especially on the internet". When I think of what the "white old male" stands for, I imagine it stereotypically as part of some sort of fraternity, or male-only bond, attached to power and prestige, not keen to share such power with others—especially with women.

But again, my father, my brother, my partner, many of my friends are white males—some older, others that will become "white old males" as time goes by. "These are the people who helped me get where I am today, so I don't think it's fair or right to completely berate them". We need to have nuances in our narrative—because reality is nuanced, I add. "Yes, we must recognise how they helped us in the past, because I wouldn't be here if it wasn't for all these males who believe in me: they created an incredible foundation for me to be me, to break every stereotype and leverage their research. Most of my mentors were male and they took that opportunity within their selves to realise that we need more representation and more ideas and to give me the support to bring just that. People will be supportive if they want to be supportive, and that's what we need to understand to break down siloes between men and women—creating strong bonds between us. We should look at people who care and people who don't care, not only at age, gender or skin colour as a way of classifying people. And that's where my dad, and my male teachers and mentors played a huge role, in caring and being supportive of my dreams and ambitions, in showing up as allies—that's what we need more of".

I see this pattern returning in how Gitanjali analyses problems. A pattern of thinking constructively instead of in a destructive manner, of highlighting the nuances rather than the stereotypes, of holding tight to hope and not to anger—a pattern I wish I would see more of in today's polarised society and media. And a pattern which could unblock the keys to changing our world. "It's a job for all of us to fix what happened to our planet!", she adds. "It's our collective world and each of us should take the collective responsibility to care for it and do what is right. Whether that's small or big. Whether that's a kind gesture or inventing a device to fix the ozone hole, there is always something you can do—and that is what really matters, what you do, how you care for others. That's what defines you as a leader. Not your gender, or age or culture".

CURIOSITY: A WAY OF LIFE

Caring, kindness, but even more being action-oriented and getting things done come back as key traits for leaders in Gitanjali's words. She tells me though that we still need to speak about the traits she values the most, or at least that she thinks are most urgently needed within our companies and countries. "I would say: being resilient and hot-headed. The willingness to push stereotypes and society expectations, that's so important", she states gesticulating, to emphasise her point. "The next thing is creativity and novelty—which wouldn't be lacking if only we had more women in leadership roles. And one of the biggest traits I feel is missing in today's leaders is risk-taking ability: taking that first step, that first risk, is what gets you further than anyone has so far. I think those are the traits of a good innovator, who to me is a good leader, a true change-maker". She looks up and quickly adds a last sentence, "It goes without saying that you need a scientific mindset, but you must have passion, drive, resilience, risk-taking capacity, to go somewhere. If you have that, then you are there, you are an innovator within yourself and you will make a real difference for our world".

Gitanjali is herself an innovator, and a leader, and these are the traits that got her through hiccups and failures over the past years—because no one progresses without facing difficulties. "Not everybody believes in me . . . many didn't and still don't believe in what I do. There will always be these people, and we must learn to deal with them. Regarding this, I want to share a story. Can I?", she asks looking at the clock, as her flying class is getting closer and closer. I nod but she has already started speaking: "When I was 10 or 11 years old, I tried for the first time to get into a lab. I wanted to start testing my lead-detection device, for safe water. I literally sent hundreds and hundreds of emails and got hundreds of negative answers. Some were a simple 'no'; some said that my ideas didn't make any sense, that I am too young for this, that I have no real goal in mind, that I am just messing around, and that I needed to have concrete ideas and extra years under my belt before getting into a lab". She looks straight into the camera, making eye contact: "It was so difficult for me, because I couldn't get more concrete ideas if not by going into a lab, learning, and testing things—but they wouldn't let me in until I had more concrete ideas, so it was a vicious cycle. And it was hard to deal with the rejection—it was the first time I had witnessed backlash as a kid. I felt people clearly thinking 'who do you think you are that you email us at this hour asking us for help?'. It was absolutely discouraging, and I had to dig deep for my resilience and to feel hot-headed in order to not lose my determination and perseverance—that's what got me through these hundreds of 'no's".

Gitanjali explains that the first time a lab reached out was only after she had gained name recognition—namely her *TIME* magazine cover. "I am fortunate to have had that chance, which opened the doors to an opportunity that changed my life: the moment I walked into that lab, I understood exactly what I wanted to do, be a scientist. But all kids should have that opportunity, not only the few like me who get name recognition. I must say, though, even with the name recognition, I still struggle with pushback or out-of-place comments. I remember the first time I ever did an interview. I sat down after giving a speech and was imagining they would ask me 'how did it feel, how is the audience in reality'. Instead, the first question they asked was 'why do you dress three times older than your age?'—I just couldn't believe it. Also a few months ago, I was asked again, 'You are 17, why do you wear a business coat, not a dress?' I was once told I am too pretty to be an innovator—they literally said, 'You could do so much more with your life—why don't you?' They comment on my nails, my looks, not what I have to say. I appreciate the compliments, don't get me wrong, but this is just crazy. All these things you see on TV, on social media, they are real: people actually think this way, have that mindset—even today". She suddenly goes silent and looks a bit shocked, "Wow", she tells herself, "it's really messed up". She looks at me and states that it's the actress syndrome: "A lot of times when I am doing something, or I am speaking, my words are not listened to just because I am a girl, because I am young, because I am South-East Asian . . . I have so much insight I want to share, but it's very, very difficult to get that legitimacy and attention. But you must deal with it, and just move on—find that internal strength and purpose and follow it, no matter what people say".

SUCCESS IS THE CAPSTONE TO A PYRAMID OF FAILURES

We continue discussing these "behind the scenes" events that Gitanjali and so many other girls and women must deal with, including myself. You might see us on a cover page, or in an interview, but life is not as pretty as a magazine cover—there are many obstacles, and lots of hard work, hidden behind any smiling picture.

"It takes years and years of work, of hard work, to get to that one picture. I am still working every single day of my life, while trying my best to be myself. From the outside, I know some think that I am working too hard, that I am intimidating. I heard people saying 'she is acting so much more mature than her age, or she is doing all these experiments while I am sitting at home not doing anything with my life'. But I want to tell people that's not what it is: I am a girl doing what she loves and my goal is to be inspiring, not discouraging, because I am confident that anyone can find their passion and dive into it as deep as I do. And to reassure you, I am a typical high school student: yes, I hang out with my friends, and yes, I am obsessed with Taylor Swift. It's just me—I wasn't fed anything strange growing up or told to do weird stuff, I am just being myself—I am a teenager doing what she loves and that's my biggest superpower, what makes me *me*—and that includes tonnes of failures and setbacks".

Gitanjali turns around and starts looking for something in her bedroom. She doesn't seem to find it, so starts speaking again, explaining that her dad recently put a quote next to her bed—while she was sleeping—the night after some disappointing news. "It was something like 'success is the capstone to a pyramid of failures'. I had some success, otherwise, I wouldn't be talking to you today—but this is truly that, the capacity to see failure as another step to success. Failure to me is messing up when it doesn't matter versus messing up when it does. Take those opportunities and, when you fail, use it to learn, to grow better ideas, to start thinking more logically, so you can become a better innovator, enhancing your capacity to lead and bring change within this world".

She starts playing with a small piece of paper on her desk and with her eyes focused on that, she adds, "No one has an amazing idea the first time around—when you are young this is incredibly discouraging, but you must understand that you live and you learn, and failure is something you can't avoid—and if you do avoid it, or you don't learn from it, it will make everything so much worse because you won't be growing as you could. I am proud to say that I failed more times than I succeeded, because it makes me the person I am: all my failures led to one success—regardless of how big or small that success is!" She takes a quick break, to then share a last thought: "You know what? Curiosity. Yes, curiosity is what above all keeps me going, and what I think a real leader should have. This desire to learn, to grow, to explore, to make mistakes, but still stay curious and keep going. If you are curious, you are resilient, you are humble, you grow faster, and you become a good leader. And that's what I hope I'll always keep with me, rooting me as a leader, whatever my future may look like: my curiosity".

"How do you imagine your future?", I ask. She knows, once more, exactly what she wants to say: "For a very long time, my dream was Forbes' 30 under 30—I saw you were also on the list?", I nod and we take a second to cheer each other up. "I am the youngest ever—I was 12", says Gitanjali with pride in her eyes. "It was wild—I was looking at the list and thought, 'Wow, I am too young for this! I hit my peak and I am 12, what am I going to do next?' Which is not a great thing to be thinking as a 12-year old to be honest. So . . . I was like 13, now what? 14, now what? 15, now what? But finally, I can tell you it's working out. My dreams have evolved: I want to create my own biotech company. I don't know what my product would be, but something around using genetic engineering and bioengineering to solve energy problems, working with science and innovation to make sustainable living and clean energy for all a reality one day. That's my goal: let's see how far that gets me. But for now, I must choose which college to go to. Of course, I'll keep dreaming, but I also just want to enjoy that chapter of my life, being just another college student!" Gitanjali looks at her clock and says she needs to run. "Otherwise I'll miss the final flying lesson". We quickly discuss next steps and say a quick goodbye, both thanking each other for the time we took for this interview, with warm smiles on our faces.

I disconnect, shut down my computer, and find it somehow odd to be in my small office room in Italy—realising I had forgotten about the distance that had made me a little anxious just a few hours before. In a couple of hours, Gitanjali and I built a bridge through our commonalities. Above all, as two optimistic, chatty, and curious women—which is probably what makes us resilient, capable of breaking boundaries, of bringing that novelty our world needs more of. I tell myself that just as the two of us managed to do it, despite the difference in our cultures, backgrounds, age, or fields of work, we must all get better at doing just that: working across professional sectors, generations, countries, for a common goal. And I tell myself that maybe the stronger bonds we wish to see among women, and between women and men, could be built exactly around this: not our roles, or the power we hold, but around the change we want to see. Because this would be the strongest bond of all.

• 3 •

CONSISTENCY
Becky Sauerbrunn

YOU KNOW THOSE KIDS who were never any good, or motivated, or interested in sports? That's me. Of course, I always did sports because I had no choice—three times per week was the minimum mandatory requirement imposed by my parents up to age 18. And that wasn't the only requirement: it had to be a sport that my brother and I could both do at the same time, to maximise the logistics efficiency of the van der Esch family. Karate, swimming, horse riding, volleyball. I did manage to convince my brother at age seven to do figure skating, but it didn't last long: after less than a year, we were back to swimming. And then there were the skiing holidays and the summer camps: all day tennis, sailing, swimming. My nightmare.

I know: I realise as I am writing these words that it sounds amazing and I am an idiot to complain—but it just wasn't for me. I did it, I wasn't bad, but never particularly good either: I lacked motivation, I didn't feel energised, I was of course competitive and would be pissed each time (i.e. always) I didn't win or outperform others—starting from my brother, but that wasn't enough to get rid of my underlying disinterest.

And it wasn't only about playing sports, it was also about watching sports. Apart from figure ice-skating, which I could spend hours watching, I remember looking confused at my dad glued to the screen watching the Olympics, or at friends spending their Sundays cheering for the local football team. I just didn't get it. One data point says it all: despite being Italian, I grew up without ever cheering for a particular football team and without ever going to a stadium to watch a match.

But I do remember clearly thinking one thing: those sports are for boys. On TV it was men competing. At the local football club, there was no girls' team. At the pool, there was water polo for boys. And, at volleyball matches between schools, we girls were replaced by the guys because they were taller and better—they were our chance to win. And now, I cannot help wondering if my attraction to figure skating was driven by this: the only sport in which—be it in my village or on TV—I saw people like me: girls and women, performing and competing.

Luckily my sports story is very far from Becky's. And the results show: she is the captain of the United States national football ("soccer", for Americans) team, won one gold and one bronze Olympic medal, two world cups, and was awarded an infinite number of best player and best defender of the year awards; on my side, I am still struggling to motivate myself to do a 15-minute workout at home three times per week.

This discrepancy between Becky and I reveals a lot, when I come to think of it: the power of passion, which I lack and Becky has for sports, but also the power of role models and supporters.

THE POWER OF ROLE MODELS

"I was 14 when the 1999 women's World Cup was held in the United States", says Becky. "I was already playing soccer in my club, and one of the mums took her daughter and a few of us teammates to watch the US-Nigeria match. She put us in a car on a hot summer day, and we drove all the way from St. Louis, where I grew up, to Chicago—it was the closest they were going to be to us, and we simply couldn't miss it". As Becky starts sharing this story, I already see a spark in her eyes. "It was the first women's game of the national team I had seen live. We enter this huge stadium, the Chicago Bears, and it's completely packed. I look around and see people's faces are painted, their chests are painted. All are cheering their asses off, watching this team scoring goals against Nigeria. To me, as a soccer fan, this was the coolest thing I had ever seen: witnessing so many other people loving soccer and watching this group of women dominating the game, while clearly enjoying being on the field and around each other. This became a seminal moment of my life. I was glued to the TV for the rest of the 1999 World Cup. Still remember watching the final match, which we won in such a sports cliche way: the final kick won the US team the cup; Brandi Chastain [the player who scored the winning penalty] ripped her shirt off; the celebrations, the happiness was just incredible. That's when I decided I'll do everything in my power to know what it feels like to be on that field, to be part of a team like that one, to achieve and celebrate such a win. That World Cup was the moment I realised I wanted to pursue soccer for as far as it would be able to take me. And, in that moment, the national team became my absolute dream, drive, and ambition".

Becky continued training, playing, improving, focused on her goal: reaching the top team of her country. "Soccer became a real door opener for me. I found amazing people along the way, ready to coach me, support me, believe in my dream. Soccer basically paid for my college education, helped me get amazing people in my life—including Zola [her partner, whom Becky met while playing soccer for the University of Virginia]—and is now my livelihood. If I think about all the amazing things that happened because of soccer, I sometimes have a hard time believing it".

Her career has indeed been phenomenal—part of the under 16, under 19, under 23, and US senior national teams, while playing in all sorts of professional clubs: from Boston to Washington, Kansas to Portland, with a detour through Norway. And one thing got her through it all: consistency.

"I am not particularly fast. I'm not particularly tall. I am also not as strong as other defenders. It is not my physical ability that got me where I am, but my capacity to show up, every single day. To be consistent. And to do so while reading the game, understanding our weaknesses, leveraging our strengths, and solving problems", explains Becky with clarity and modesty. "It is this consistency in my mindset, in my attitude, in training what is under my control, that has allowed me to develop as a player, to transform into a leader, and to get where I am today".

COMFORTABLE WITH THE UNCOMFORTABLE

"What sports can teach anybody", explains Becky "is that most of the time things are just out of your control: the weather, the referee, the other team. The only thing that you are in control of at any moment is yourself and your attitude. It's your work ethic, your decision-making. And it's a very uncomfortable place to be in, to realise there are only a few elements you can be in control of and that everything else is an X factor. So, your best option is to adapt, to make decisions on the go, in a direction that will hopefully positively influence the outcome—despite all the unknown forces surrounding you".

Being comfortable with the uncomfortable has never been my strength. Adaptability, problem-solving, rapid decision-making is, but it is a way of getting out of the uncomfortable—not of sitting with it. I ask Becky how she built this comfort, this resilience, to sit with what feels uncomfortable. "The best way is by fostering an environment that basically does that to you.

In every training session, in every meeting, there should be an element of being uncomfortable: whether it is physically, or mentally, even psychologically. An element which is there, but in a measured and healthy way, helping you create an environment in which you can never feel complacent—because you never know what's going to happen next—and slowly learn to sit and deal better with this uncomfortable feeling, becoming more resilient within it".

Becky explains that in soccer, this is something you often do during the evaluation phase: after trainings, matches, victories, and defeats, the team meets to evaluate how it went, to watch "film" (as Becky calls it—i.e. the replay of the match for non-soccer-experts). "It's crucial to feel there's always something to learn. You're never going to be perfect, not even when you win the best match of your life, but you can be appreciative of the progress you make as you strive for excellence, understand where you fall short, and make corrections. I call this overall feeling the 'wholesome discontent', it helps you get a little bit more comfortable with the uncomfortable so that when you get to very high-pressure moments, such as the World Cup, you can tell yourself, 'I have been here before, I've felt this pressure, this discomfort, and I survived it'. That is what keeps you going in the hardest and most high-pressure moments, and that capacity can be built only over time".

Mistakes also play a role in Becky's "wholesome discontent" approach. Since in sports, the concept that mistakes are bad is a concept which simply doesn't apply if you want to be at the highest level. "Inherently, mistakes are made constantly when you're playing. Instead of being afraid of those mistakes, the best strategy is to embrace them, use them as tools to learn from. That's the only chance in sports to get better: your mistakes and other people's mistakes. Observe them, treasure them, take responsibility for your own mistakes, and be able to feel safe in calling someone out when they make a mistake—to understand why they made it, how they felt, learn something about that person in the process, and help anyone in the team make sure they don't repeat the same mistake twice. This honest and vulnerable environment is the best chance any team has for success. On the national team, we call this 'sharing your scars'—and I think this is something unique we have in the sports world, which could maybe help other workforces to learn, adapt, and perform better".

Becky's articulation of her thoughts, processing of her and her teams' experiences, clarity on what she has learned from each one of them, and capacity to progress in a consistent and reliable way—as an athlete and as a person—are a testament to this spirit of constant learning she describes. And this is one of the key traits that coaches and managers saw in her early on, and so encouraged Becky to step up to leadership positions.

IMPOSTORS, EVEN WHILE LEADING

"The first time I perceived myself as a leader was not because I thought I was one or because I aspired to be one, but because I was told by the coaching staff they saw potential in me. It was 2014, going into the 2015 World Cup, which was going to be the last tournament for our national team co-captains who were phasing out of their career. It felt flattering to be identified as a potential future captain, but I was also unsure of how to develop into a leader. I was told I should speak more, as they needed to hear my voice during the team meetings and on the field, and for the group to start getting used to me playing such a role. I was then appointed as a co-captain in 2016, at a difficult time for the team. Things were souring between the players and the technical/coaching staff, and I tried to bridge the gap between the two, which is what a captain should do, but felt alone and unsure in this process. I remember very clearly telling myself that I was appointed captain and I should be able to take the situation in my hands, rectify it, but what I really felt was insecure, felt like an impostor who was failing miserably at doing that. Instead of leaning on people, empowering them, asking for help, instead of being myself, I tried to be strong, decisive, and determined. I wasn't sure what to do and ended up relying a lot on external advice, which probably turned out to be one of the worst pieces of advice I had received so far: it made me get into my head, not out of my head, it made me turn inwards, not reach out to others, it helped create a situation of isolation, rather than of team spirit. And that became a huge blowback: I moved away from who I am, the environment became unwelcoming, unappealing, the situation became way more stressful than it needed to be, I felt alone in it all, and it simply became untenable".

Many people suffer from impostor syndrome. And data confirms women suffer from it more often than men. A KPMG study, focusing on the US, found that 75% of female executives across all sorts of industries have experienced it in their careers. They felt anxious, incapable of experiencing success internally despite their objective high performance: just as Becky felt, despite being a top world football player winning an infinite number of awards at national and international level.

This feeling can be triggered by a range of situations and circumstances. One of these is feeling (or simply looking) different from the others who have made it, because of race, gender, age, religion, sexual orientation, or other factors. Those who suffer impostor syndrome feel out of place or, in extreme cases, a fraud. Whenever we face a new challenge, impostor syndrome whispers "I am not ready", while a growth mindset would say, "I'll get myself ready for it". This is why such syndrome can lead to negative coping mechanisms and behaviours, sometimes getting people stuck into vicious cycles.

Becky lost the captain role in 2018. And felt like a failure. "But again", she says, "going back to mistakes, it's something from which I learned a lot. I know better now: what is important is to empower others, to create a sounding board of people you can lean on around you, to be able to ask for help when needed, and to be myself—with all my strengths and vulnerabilities. I tried to lead by being someone else and that backfired, and now that I am captain again, I am applying what I learned the hard way and hoping for better results. Leadership in the end is this: promoting people's strengths while diminishing each other's weaknesses—which applies also to who is leading. And doing so in a way that we're complementing each other, making the journey a little bit easier towards what we're trying to accomplish".

Becky opens up on how her idea of leadership evolved with time. "I would say that the thing that's probably evolved the most, from when I first entered a leadership position to now, is my awareness of the fact that you can never undervalue the compassion aspect, the human-to-human part of leadership". Relationships, trust, capacity to rely on one another are a core component of any functional and performing team. "This aspect is much more important than the top-down, in-your-face, 'I'm telling you what to do' type of leadership. I recently realised something: appointed leaders see themselves as people who know what they're doing, should be able to delegate, to tell people how they can do something faster. And this is an entirely wrong way of doing it. If you actually want to get somewhere faster, with a better relationship, and a better experience, if you want to get to that mountaintop, what I found is that the human element and the capacity to leverage other people's strengths—not only your own, makes the journey that much more enjoyable, enriching, and efficient. Compassion is key. Authenticity is key. All while showing up in a consistent way, for yourself and for others. This is the meaning of leadership to me".

ON THE FIELD

"How does this leadership style look like on the field?", I ask Becky, curious to get insights from this faraway world for me. "Captains have very different roles depending on what the team needs at the time, and this is an important starting point: your team's needs, not yours. For example, our head coach—whom I had worked with in Kansas City—just got announced a few years ago, and it was his first time coaching the national team. This means a big part of my job has been building a bridge between him, his technical staff, and us players. Being a conduit means making sure I know what he's trying to do—i.e., how he foresees the team to play, how he wants the team to be off the field—I help explain that to the players, all while fostering that relationship between player and coach—as a group and as individual athletes. And I try and do this while still being very true to what the players need". I ask Becky what she means by that. "In order for us to be at our best, we can be very picky. Different players need different things. I know the players well enough to understand these things, know when someone is struggling, and bridge that gap with the coach to ensure our team performs at its best and wins".

It seems to be a conciliatory role, trying to move the team, the game, in the right direction while keeping everyone on board. "What happens when you and the head coach disagree?", I ask. "Oh", says Becky while laughing, "it happens all the time. And I am convinced that's part of a healthy relationship. It's never disrespectful: he'll hear my opinion, I'll hear his. The head coach understands that I am the players' captain, which means my moral compass is pointed towards what's best for the group, for the players' health and happiness, and I'm skewed that way. And that understanding my role towards the team alleviates any stress or anxiety that comes from disagreements: we each stand for something, and we are both trying to do our jobs as best as we can. Of course", continues Becky with a smile on her face, "if we really can't agree, at the end he is the head coach and I fall in line, because that's my job".

Something that fascinates me when watching sports as a spectator is this capacity to hold together a team, of playing this "conciliatory" card, with the parallel infinite layers of competitiveness. Every player is competing to be the best, to score the most goals, to run the fastest, also within the same team. In parallel, every team is competing to win against the other. And sometimes, this competition is among players (e.g. in a World Cup) who are your teammates on a normal basis (e.g. in the club and not national team compositions). You see this fierce competition, but at the end of the game, you see players from opposite teams coming back together.

"I am very well aware that yourself and the other women you interviewed for this book have real stakes in their jobs, with real lives on the line. So I am now speaking exclusively of the sports arena. Competition is fierce, and it's part of everything we do—within and between teams: getting on the national team, staying on the national team, beating other national teams. But as a team captain, I have my own way of managing that". I ask her to tell me more. "At our level of sports, we are in high-pressure situations all the time: anxiety, tension are simply part of it. And as a team, we can either decide to make that environment even more stressful, by being unwelcoming to each other, or to make it a little smoother. Many of the environments I have been part of—including the national team in the past—were adding and not decreasing stress. But I think that's the wrong way to go: if we succeed in creating an environment in which you have a psychological safety net to fall back on within your team, it's going to improve team performance and increase competitiveness externally. Two simple reasons: knowing your teammates care and value you as an athlete but also as a person will make you perform better; and feeling freer to be vulnerable within your team, thanks to this safety net, will remove your fear of failing and make you dare more during games—which will, in turn, generate better results, lifting our team's competitiveness level towards the outside world higher and higher. In short, better human connections on the inside generate a better performance on the outside".

I write that down and, when I look back up at Becky, I notice she has got a big smile. She is thinking of her team's victories. "Oh man", she says, "when you win, with this team spirit, it will be a completely different feeling. I still remember the 2015 World Cup victory: it was my first one, I was in the field the moment we won—my childhood dream became a reality. After initial celebrations on the field, the real ones started in the locker room. Drinking champagne, beer, feeling this group of women I have just suffered with, lived with, basically done everything with throughout this tournament is now celebrating its success. It is celebrating this rare instance of being the last team winning, of seeing your journey, for once, getting you to that mountaintop. Those moments are rare and have the power to make all the long training hours, injuries, frustrations, suddenly disappear".

My instinctive reaction to Becky's career highlight during the 2015 World Cup is to think that it must feel exciting but also scary to reach your peak so young. "It is and it isn't", says Becky in a reassuring tone. "You're in the locker room, you're celebrating, it's a lot of happiness, it's a lot of relief. But you are already looking for the next mountain top: the Olympics in 2016, the next World Cup in 2019, and now we are looking to the World Cup this summer (2023). I never feared not being able to achieve that same height, I was simply getting ready to achieve whatever was coming next. And that's the mindset I appreciate of my team, of sports: there is no complacency, we don't relax because we won one World Cup, but rather focus on winning three in a row—which I hope will become a reality soon", she concludes with a fiery competitive look in her eyes.

Becky's team is preparing for the upcoming World Cup. And this requires alternating between two modes and speeds of life: being "out of camp", i.e. in your professional club, playing a few hours per day, and then recovering for the next day; and being "in camp"—i.e. with the national team, living together, eating together, training like crazy, and having constant meetings to improve strategy and performance. "The difference between being a national team player and a professional player isn't so much about a person's skill level, it is about their ability to survive and thrive in the very stressful environment on camp. And it took me a long time to understand how to do that".

LEADING AS AN INTROVERT

Becky is an introvert, and she speaks openly about the difficulty of finding her way and her place in a team of extroverts. "For a long time, I didn't really understand introversion enough and was not able to put into words how I felt when constantly surrounded by people: as if energy was being sucked out of my soul. I didn't quite understand why I wanted to be alone more often than not. And I convinced myself this was strange, abnormal. Until I read a book which was life altering, and which I would recommend to all introverts: *Quiet* by Susan Cain. That's the moment I learned I am normal, I am simply an introvert in a team of people longing to be together, party, bond—because they are extroverts. Understanding that allowed me to become aware of my need to set boundaries and put myself into a space where I can relax, especially during high-pressure moments. And, with time, I've gotten strategic in protecting my space, at finding the power of saying, 'no, I can't do this right now, but I'll get to it later'. I carve out little but crucial moments to recharge and to ensure I'll be at my best when I actually have to do something important. I just wished though I would have learned that earlier, not just a couple of years ago. It made me unhappy, misunderstood—by myself and by others, and it created stress and anxiety especially during my teenage years, which perhaps I could have avoided. Understanding my introversion at a younger age would have made me feel more settled with myself, confident, and this is why I share my story—hoping it can help younger women identify these traits and be reassured that they are completely normal".

I find her words fascinating. As a full-on extrovert, I often struggle to understand why certain people—starting from my partner—need to retreat, be by themselves. Even if I rationally tell myself that it's just a different character, I can't help not thinking there is something wrong with what I have done or said, or with them, whenever they retreat. So as Becky shares her experience, I write down: "Note to self: it's OK, just let them be". As I am finishing the note, Becky starts speaking again. "In that book, there's a part about leadership as an introvert, especially relevant when you are the leader of an extroverted group. It means being an observer, a fly on the wall: you see players having all these ideas, exploring 2000 different tactics, while I'm just sitting there, watching people, soaking in everyone's best points, taking the temperature of the room, to then put it together into something that is cohesive, which can work during the game and make us successful. I didn't appreciate the strength of being an introverted leader until after reading that book. And now I am proud of playing the role of a thermostat: keeping everything even keeled, making sure we never get too high or too low, staying at the right temperature to be productive".

Becky's framing of keeping the team in this productive space is a concept I learned in a leadership class at Harvard and which—despite having managed many teams—I had not put into words myself before hearing it in class. And it's a concept that is particularly relevant for those trying to bring change, while ensuring their survival: if you raise the temperature too high, people will try and get rid of you and you will no longer succeed in bringing change, and if the temperature is too low, change won't happen. And this awareness of the right middle is one of the key factors behind Becky's achievements on and off the field.

MAKING HISTORY, BEYOND THE FIELD

Indeed, in addition to leading her team, she is a change-maker, a trailblazer, off the field as well. Becky won't acknowledge it openly, because she is too modest (not like the fake modest people—who say they didn't do something to be told by others they did; she is a real modest one—which gets red cheeks the moment you hint at her merit), but with a few colleagues they made history. Not for winning the World Cup, this time, but for securing equal pay for female athletes in her country.

It was March 2016 when, along with four other colleagues from the national team, Becky filed a complaint with the Equal Employment Opportunity Commission of the United States, about wage discrimination as compared to the men's national team. What helped the US national team was their decision to unionise under a players' association, to collectively bargain for their wages and working conditions. Becky was elected by fellow players to represent them in the negotiations with the US Soccer Federation and was nominated the first president of this association in 2020—leading them into a mediatic lawsuit and historical bargaining agreement in 2022, securing equal pay.

"To have achieved equal pay feels amazing and surreal. I didn't believe it was going to happen during my career, so I was just pursuing the fight that female players before me had started, to make it a little bit fairer and easier for future generations of players. The fact that us, the current group, got to push across the line made me feel proud, as this was a game changer for women in the US. Not only in sports", Becky adds in a hopeful voice. "Others, in the US and internationally, can now point at us, look at how we achieved equal pay, and use this to affirm their rights, their equal treatment, at work and beyond".

"Change is often incremental", says Becky, "which is frustrating because you want it to be exponential". As she spells out these words, I think back to all the times when I felt that exact frustration, as I wanted to turn things upside down but couldn't, because true change often happens slowly, and you must be patient and persistent enough if you want to make it happen. "Our victory might seem like a sudden shift in equal pay rights from the outside, but it is not. Many generations of women players fought for a liveable wage first and then kept pushing that ceiling higher and higher until we got to crash it with our current team. But even for us, it was no easy task".

Viewership of women's sports in the US is at 4%. Peanuts. Becky explains they are an up-and-coming marketplace, in which no one is willing to invest though—which makes any change much harder to achieve. "It feels we are constantly navigating a thin line: balancing our requests for better wages, working conditions, while realising that if we ask for too much, investors are ready to let the league fold: their pockets and buy-in are limited compared to the men's league. It's an art to find that balance, to make sure we can stick around while trying to push for progress and equality. But now that we have made it happen, I see our achievement at a national level as a solid starting point to continue pushing, to make sure this is applied to the professional clubs, for national teams in other countries. We are working with a few of them to help achieve just that", explains Becky as she lists the teams—Germany, Canada, Spain—who have approached her since this landmark case, to use the strategies and arguments adopted in the US within their countries.

"I wish I could do more though. Equal pay is key, but there are so, so, so many other barriers that stop us from accessing equal opportunities. Barriers that girls and women face since the moment they are born. Be it education, healthcare, safety. These are the reasons why we are struggling to get into the upper ranks, into the decision-making rooms: we're simply not getting access to equal opportunities from the get-go. We start from a deficit, behind the starting line where most men are. Having us all at the same starting block—women and men— seems such a basic thing, but it's not what happens in today's world. And I want to play my role in changing this".

Becky's voice is energetic, full of drive, purpose, as she explains how she is taking forward these battles, along with her team-mates. "I would say that my purpose is still an ongoing journey", says Becky with a shade of shyness in her voice. "When I first got into the national team, I was here for the ride. Then I started meeting women who stood up, who fought for what they believed in, who asked the right questions . . . and I realised that I was brainwashed: I didn't even realise there were these problems, let alone that I could or should do something about it. You know . . .", continues Becky as her eyes look reflective, "you almost need to be reprogrammed, to see what you couldn't see. Being surrounded by these strong opinionated women allowed me to start seeing: realising I was asking the wrong questions or, even worse, I was not asking questions at all. These women helped me find and refine my moral compass—especially Megan".

Megan Rapinoe, the iconic winger and former captain of the US national soccer team (whose fame also transformed her into a Barbie and a Lego icon), is a close friend of Becky—and one of the people who shaped her the most. "I call her Pino", she says with a sweet smile on her face, "and we are kind of

a ying and yang. She is an extrovert, I am an introvert, she is
outspoken and loves the limelight, I avoid it. We met at age
16—oh gosh", she says with a baffled face while doing a quick
calculation in her head, "20 years ago—wow! As all friend-
ships, we had periods in which we drifted apart, periods when
it got stronger. But throughout this journey, she made me
braver: I watched and learned as she was standing up for what
she believes in, going to HBO specials, hosting panels. And
I probably helped her as well, to be more curious and nuanced
when approaching others, the world. Pino and I spent infinite
hours discussing how it can be beneficial for an introvert to
be a leader, as a cohesion point for the bunch of extroverts
we have within our team. And of how important it is not to
diminish the value of having both perspectives. Because this
is what we are, what we bring to each other and to the team:
opposite personalities, complementary perspectives. I couldn't
have achieved what I have without her support, her guidance,
her swag".

She explains that at first, it felt uncomfortable, as an introvert, to use her own voice, step into the spotlight, question
the status quo. "Getting comfortable with the uncomfortable
is something I know how to do when it comes to sports",
says Becky, "so I tried to replicate the same mechanism to
finding my voice and leading off the field. And it worked: by
now, I feel comfortable in being vocal, in standing for what
I believe in—if I managed to do such a fundamental shift,
it means anyone can do it, also those reading these words
and feeling hesitant, insecure, about their capacity to do just
that. Today, if I see an injustice, and I sit with it and it feels
wrong, I know I have to say something, I must act, or I will
regret it. We need to ask questions, fight for the right things.
For acceptance and belonging as opposed to marginalising

or diminishing people. This is why I feel I'm fighting for the right things, and this inner conviction makes it a lot easier to step into uncomfortable situations".

LEADERSHIP, POWER, DIVERSITY: A TRIAD FOR CHANGE

Becky takes a quick break and then continues speaking, shifting the focus from herself to the rest of the world. "It scares me to see people in decision-making positions, in power, being the same type of people", she says. "If I look at our US Soccer Federation, our board has been historically made up of older white cisgender privileged males. If I look at government, the same. And things don't change much when you look at CEOs in the corporate world". She takes a deep breath as she explains that what scares her is seeing that, despite knowing we need to get diversity in the ranks, those in power do everything they can to hold onto that power and not share it. "To the detriment of the people they're supposed to be leading, representing, or working for".

Holding onto power is a trait that many develop once they get into powerful positions, and it's not exclusive to men. "It's important to understand this", says Becky while nodding, agreeing to my point. "I've seen many women stepping up the ladder, into power positions, but then holding onto this power without creating space for others to go up that same ladder. It's understandable, it's human: it's the first time they've ever had such power and instead of making the pie bigger, they focus on their slice of the pie, making it exclusive to them, protecting it from those who want to share it. We need women to bring the diversity at top levels, but ideally, we need them also to be willing to share that success, leverage it to empower others. Because the diversity we bring should comprise a capacity to style a new type of leadership, not simply reproducing the old—and often dysfunctional—one. A collaborative, empathetic style, driven by the impact we want to have and not by power per se—because these are traits that we can and do bring to the table when we are not fearful of others, and these are the traits needed to fix our companies and our countries".

As Becky describes the leadership style women can and should bring to the table, I immediately think of two role models of mine, who, from my point of view, perfectly embed Becky's words: Jacinda Ardern, former prime minister of New Zealand, and Nicola Sturgeon, former prime minister of Scotland. Not only have they been styling new traits of leadership, but they also showed an attachment and a loyalty to the change they want and can bring, rather than power per se. To the point that they stepped down from power, not because they had to, they were defeated, but because they felt they were no longer better placed to advance change: both Ardern and Sturgeon left space for someone new to step in and step up in advancing the change they want to see.

On top of this underlying problem of power, i.e. wanting to maintain it no matter what, there is a second problem among today's "leaders", according to Becky. Their limited capacity to understand people or groups which are different from themselves: those who historically have not held power, who have been discriminated against or marginalised, most times by those in power trying to preserve their exclusivity on it. "The lack of compassion, of empathy, of sympathy for someone that's different from yourself, your family, your in-group is another thing that really scares me", says Becky with an urgency and preoccupation I hadn't yet heard in her voice. "Decisions, at the highest levels, are being taken based on how they favour those in power and not based on how they help the majority of us, let alone those marginalised. Politics has become transactional, selfish. As if the human element was removed from it, and the focus—when voting, when governing—is on how each of us can get ahead, rather than how we can make life better for all people". Becky takes a quick pause, as she is gathering her thoughts, and then goes on: "This is exactly why I would like those in leadership positions to be more curious, open-minded, ready to learn about people who are different from them. Too many do the opposite, they lead with fear, which simply hides an ignorance, an unwillingness to embrace things that you don't know. An initial lack of curiosity leads to a lack of compassion, which then makes it so much easier to do horrendous things to those who don't look or think like you—be it through legislations, through bans, through violation of their rights, through war—because they are seen as lesser, as scary, because they are not understood for what they are: human beings, with the same rights we all have".

As politics is always becoming more polarised, sports has the power to do the opposite: break down divisions, barriers. By bringing people together around a common activity, ambition, game within and across communities, religions, social classes, nations. "Soccer is a sport that lifts people up. Without it, a lot of the top players would have never had a chance to reach the type of work, income, fame that they have, moving beyond their original social class, country. It's the same for me: many of the opportunities I now have come from sports, many doors opened because of it, and this is why to me it is important to pay this forward. Trying to make it more accessible to groups of people that have been marginalised, don't have the same opportunities, but that—just as I did—could learn and grow by discovering and following their passion for soccer. This is what motivates me, what really excites me, and how I want to use the platform I currently have as an elite athlete: to lift others up".

DREAMS IN A DRAWER

Elite athletes though reach their peak young. And Becky, now 37, is reaching the age of having to consider what comes next, after retiring from sports. As I mention her future, I see doubt starting to fill her eyes, her tone less determined. "I've only really seen myself as a soccer player, which uses her platform to try to do good. What am I going to be once I am no longer a soccer player, and maybe I don't have that platform anymore, I really don't know. I would need to find myself again, my place, my identity in this world. And that intrigues me, scares me, excites me at the same time", she says with some hesitation in her voice, as she seems still unclear of what that would look like.

One of my favourite expressions in Italian is *un sogno nel cassetto* (i.e. a dream in a drawer). A wish, a fantasy, a dream you have kept in the drawer for a long time, maybe since you were a child, and that one day you hope will come true. I dreamed of becoming a veterinarian (as we grew up surrounded by cats, birds, fishes, and frogs), a ballerina or figure skater (wonder why?), and a cashier (because I loved selling objects in our house and hand-writing receipts). I don't think any of them will become a reality, but they were my childhood dreams. Becky says she can't think of an equivalent expression in English, but she gets the gist: "A radio DJ host—that was my big dream", she says while laughing at her own ambitions as a child. "So maybe I can convert to that, do a podcast, or something like that?", she pauses for a second and says that Zola—her partner—would be disappointed if she would end up settling for that. "He knows I could do more and, also if I don't admit it because I am getting impostor syndrome as we are speaking about my future, I also know deep down I can do more. It just all feels so uncertain . . . but what is certain to me is that I still want to be around sports and be someone who tries to bring change—*how*, I really don't know".

A second wish for her future is clear to Becky though. Not relating to what she will do, but to how she will feel about herself: no longer an impostor. "I am doing the best I can, and that's all anyone can really ask from me, or from anyone", she says as if speaking to herself, with a reassuring voice. "I am trying to learn, of course there are lots of things I still don't know, and that's okay. As long as I keep trying, while not doubting my value each time I do it". Her honesty, her inner depth, combined with her outward simplicity make me feel I am dealing with a rare gem, and I wish for a second she could see herself as I do, feeling reassured that there is absolutely no reason why she should question her value. But self-confidence has "self" in it for a reason, and as much as we can get external confirmations, it's only you, Becky, myself who can build it from within us.

External support, though, always comes in handy. And Becky has "a rock", as she describes him, to rely on: Zola. They met at university, in 2005, and have been together ever since. "Obviously it's life-changing to find your person. And not only am I lucky because I did find him, but also because I had the chance to grow up with him". As soon as she starts speaking of Zola, I perceive a difference in tone, in intensity of emotions, her eyes filled with affection and admiration. "I love the way we complement each other. I felt it already in college, when we were young and dumb, both trying to learn who we are—him an extrovert, me an introvert as it turned out.

He shares my passion for soccer, is my biggest fan, but at the same time, my biggest pusher. Zola constantly asks questions, encourages me to test and overcome my boundaries, to step into the unknown. It's his constant blanket of love which makes my failures less harsh and my successes even better, and which has allowed me over time to feel safe also when I enter the unknown. With him by my side, my post-soccer life feels immediately less scary".

Becky and I start discussing how having a solid partner standing with and by us has been and continues to be instrumental for our careers. "A man who is a lighthouse you can look up to, not a dark hole trying to drag you in; a man who is happy for you, not jealous of your success; a man who is ready to support you, not to discourage you from being yourself. That's what I have, and what every woman, every person, out there deserves. And that's why I call him my rock, my tether". As Becky continues this declaration of love for Zola, I realise her words are making me teary—because they are filled with honesty and emotions, but also because they get me thinking how lucky I also am to have found that type of man. "I am going to be forever exceedingly thankful to Zola's mum: she is a very strong person and taught him to be drawn to strength in woman, not to be threatened by it—which many men are". We both laugh, joking how crucial strong mothers can be in making life easier (or hell) to the future girlfriends and wives of their suns.

DOING WHAT OTHERS CAN'T: THE COURAGE
OF LEADERSHIP

Our lives are indeed nothing else than that: a net of deeply intertwined relationships and events. In which each of us has power on those surrounding us: shaping, lifting, or pushing them down. A power we must all be mindful of. Also considering that, as proven by Zola's mother, how we use it affects not only our life but the lives of those surrounding us, of people we are yet to meet or never will, and that of the generations to come.

"One of the best pieces of advice I ever got", says Becky, "relates to this. Soccer teams, teams in general, communities, society, are a gentle, intricate, complex ecosystem of relationships. This means that, when one person is off, it can disrupt everything else", I nod—as I have been too many times in this type of dynamic, be it at work or in my family and friend circles. "What we usually do is to accuse this person", I nod again, as I surely did it in the past. "Instead", continues Becky, "the advice I got is to approach that same person in a curious way. Understand what's going on with them, what they are dealing with, and see if we can help them overcome those difficulties. Adopting this advice has taught me a lot about leadership and about the importance of a leader to not corner someone who is negatively affecting our environment, but rather understand how to bring them back into their constructive role, in a consistent and reliable way, for the success of the team".

Showing curiosity, as Becky suggests, when someone is being disruptive is the hardest thing of all. It requires to sit back, take stock, show empathy, show willingness to listen and learn—not only to judge. It requires wisdom and patience, which—I admit—I sometimes fall short of in my personal and professional environment. But when you manage to do so, two things happen: you change the trajectory of that person, of the team, of the project you are working on—usually for the better; and it automatically creates a respect, a loyalty, a connection and admiration towards you, as a leader, which is then difficult to break—because you managed to do what no one else managed to in a moment of tension and difficulty. This skill, this wisdom, this patience, of observing, listening, connecting, to then put our shared humanity at the centre, with consistency and reliability is something Becky has within her and is probably the reason why she has evolved into a beloved captain and leader on and off the field.

With this thought in mind, I look at Becky, as I know our time is coming to an end and I want to soak in a little more of her environment. She is sitting tall in her chair, with her blond hair up in a casual bun, wearing a greyish sporty t-shirt. Behind her is a library filled with books, FIFA medals, and a pair of bright red football shoes. Her eyes speak kindness, simplicity, modesty, and intelligence. And everything she just said confirms just that.

Before saying goodbye, I feel like sharing what I thought of this interview. Something I haven't done with anyone else, but it came spontaneously. As someone whose thoughts go first through the mouth and then through the head, I realised too late what I was doing and hoped she wouldn't mind the feedback—as it was mainly compliments. It came spontaneously for two reasons: partly to reassure her, knowing she doubts herself made me want to take some of these doubts away; even more, though, to encourage her to do more and more, off the field and post-retirement. We need people with her leadership, her intellect, her perspective on the world, and also with her type of character—her introversion—to be part of the conversation: they have an observation and reflection capacity from which we can all learn enormously—starting from myself—and which could surely benefit our collective decision-making processes, often led or occupied by louder extroverted people who, like me, too often speak before thinking. The truth is that each of us—in our own way—can bring change and inspire others to do just the same, and for this to happen, it is crucial to showcase diverse models of leadership: a mould that fits us all simply doesn't exist.

As I share these words, I get a little emotional again, and I think (or imagine) she does as well. I leave the call feeling Becky and I have managed, in just a few hours, to become confidants. We shared our fears, our failures, our successes, and our dreams—the ones in the drawer and the ones we haven't dared yet to verbalise. We imagined how our world could change, and strategised on how each of us can become more effective in pushing our own boundaries to make things a little better. But, most of all, we connected as human beings, as women, as millennials, ready to stand with and by each other—despite our difference in culture, in sectors, in skills.

So much so that for the first time in my life, it feels like the most natural thing to watch the upcoming World Cup, cheering for Becky and her team every step of their way. Knowing that even if I will never get to know the feeling of being part of such a team, my future daughter or granddaughter might do, thanks to people like Becky. Role models who are pushing boundaries, stereotypes, archaic models, showcasing that following your passion and shaping your path (while demanding equal rights) is possible. It takes consistency, it takes humanity, it takes courage, it takes hard work, and most of all it takes being yourself, but it is an achievable goal, no matter whether we were born girls or boys.

· 4 ·

AUTHENTICITY

Diane von Furstenberg

by Jesse Frohman

YOU KNOW WHEN SOMEONE enters your life exactly at the right time? Diane von Furstenberg was that person for me.

I was going through a rough couple of days at work. Those type of days where everything seems to be going in the wrong direction. I felt as if I lacked energy, motivation, hope that we were going to manage to transform our organisational vision into reality, into real change on the ground—not because of anything to do with the actual work, or my team, but because of a few disruptive (due to insecurity, to feeling threatened—especially by confident and competent women colleagues) people (men, as it happens to be) in the team who managed to dominate the whole dynamic because of their senior positions. Putting the focus on them, on their power struggles, on their authority, on their role—and, by doing so, creating frustration (starting with myself, owing to short-sighted and unproductive discussions), and managing to undermine rather than amplify the work we were doing—thereby redirecting organisational energy to power and control issues rather than to actual work.

I was clear on what was happening: we were witnessing a backlash from the more old-style, more macho and actually also less competent senior managers, due to the fact that we were advancing things, female and male colleagues together, without, however, using the usual authority and control schemes of management. We were bringing change, through a different management style and interpretation of leadership itself, which created a backlash from those who see leadership as authority, as control, as power over people. And who want to feel needed, in control, respected. Sounds familiar? I am sure it does, as this is the type of backlash that we all witness when attempting to bring change. A backlash that nevertheless drains your energy when dealing with it, and makes you question if you really have sufficient persistence to continue pushing and pushing and pushing. A backlash that the leaders across these chapters faced throughout their careers, and which I was facing as part of mine. It wasn't the first time, and I knew it was not going to be the last time either. The difference though was that, for once, I was facing it while working on this book—while interviewing other leaders who went through similar experiences, and while trying to learn, from them, how to persist in leading change despite the obstacles, pushbacks and rejections.

In the midst of these bitter 48 hours, I connected to my previously scheduled interview with Diane—a welcome break from my overthinking of this work situation, from my feelings of frustration. And in just one hour, she turned my day (and perspective) around.

"Gaia . . . being a woman is hard, but it's much better than the alternative". Diane starts the interview without me even asking the first question. She has a witty and charming tone, a voice which transmits power and calmness at the same time. And the attitude of someone who is always ready to lift others up, with her stories, with a joke, or with an inspiring punchline that will stick with you for the rest of your life.

LIFE, AFTER DARKNESS

Diane was born in Brussels, 1946, to a Greek mother and a Moldovan father—both Jewish, who had migrated to Belgium in their youth. "My mother arrived as a young girl, went to school in Brussels—the same school where I then went to, but in 1942, the year before her high school graduation, she was not permitted to continue studying due to racial laws. Her headmaster allowed her to stay informally, but my mother couldn't get the official final diploma. She then decided to join the resistance—fighting against Nazism, and, long story short, was arrested and deported to Auschwitz, to the concentration camp. My mother became one of the few survivors, and the story of how she made it is just surreal: she had befriended a woman on her way to the concentration camp, and decided they would always stick together—no matter what. As they arrive at the camp, the guards start directing some to the right, others to the left. My mother and the lady are directed to opposite sides, so she decides not to obey and follow her friend—hoping the guards would not notice. A guard sees her, throws her to the ground, and then back into the opposite lane. My mother looks at that man with all the hatred she could muster. Without knowing that, by shifting lane, she had just been saved. The other lane was going directly to the gas chambers". As Diane shares this story, I feel shivers running through my back, and my work dilemma is already behind me.

"My mother weighed 29 kilos when she was liberated, in June 1945. A bunch of bones in the hashes of the genocide", says Diane as if imagining it in her head, as she must have thousands of times throughout her life. "But she survived. Once home, my grandmother fed her like a little bird for months in a row, and she regained her weight. And after six months, she got married to her fiancé. The doctor warned them not to have children, or at least not for a few years, because my mother was simply too fragile and wouldn't survive it, and the child might not be normal".

"Well", says Diane with a proud smile, "nine months later, I was born, and I was not normal".

Her birth was a triumph: Lily, Diane's mother, was not meant to survive; Diane was not meant to be born. "God saved my life so that I can give you life", Lily used to say to Diane.

"And I feel it's now my duty to make up for it all, for my mother's suffering, by celebrating freedom, by living as fully as I possibly can", says Diane as a way of explaining where her endless energy and love for life derive from.

Despite her family story of persecution and despite her curly black hair, which made her feel different from her blond classmates, Diane enjoyed a privileged childhood, as part of Brussels' high society. "My mother was so humiliated she couldn't move on to university, given racial laws didn't allow her to graduate from high school and to thereby continue studying. So, she wanted to make sure I would, and that I would get the opportunities she didn't get . . . As many women in my generation, I lived the unlived life of my mother".

Diane admits that the way she is has a lot to do with Lily. "My mother always pushed me ahead, making me stand up on my first birthday to give a speech. She always taught me fear was not an option: I still remember being put in a dark closet, because I feared the dark, and, while sitting there, discovering the dark slowly became lighter, feeling I could start seeing the objects, learning that nothing would happen to me. And lastly, my mother always raised me as if being a woman was a strength, an advantage—which shaped my perspective on what I could become".

A MAN'S LIFE IN A WOMAN'S BODY

Diane starts recounting her life story.

Boarding school in the UK, a degree in economics from the University of Geneva, a relationship with a beautiful prince, an assistant to a fashion photographer in Paris, and then an early career between needles, jerseys, and prints on the shores of Como Lake. "*Tu lo sai, sei Italiana* [You know this, as you are Italian]. . ." she says in Italian with her cute French accent, "but to those who are not: Lake Como was the end of the silk road, so it was filled with silk manufacturing and print shops—it was the dream place to be in to learn about colour, prints, materials".

Then the proposal during a spring night in Rome, the unexpected pregnancy, the last-minute Parisian wedding with her prince, and the decision to move to America to start a life and a family together. "I had been to the US before. My mother had gifted me a ticket for my birthday to go and visit Egon [von Furstenberg]—whom I had met in Geneva, for a short holiday with him. I couldn't believe it; New York was dangerous. Dirty. Cheap. It was full of artists in the streets. And it was the most inspiring thing I had ever done. My prince was invited everywhere, and I went along. The girls there weren't happy to see me—he was the bachelor everyone hoped to marry. But the designers were: I would go with Egon to the most exclusive parties, and they would dress me for these occasions. So, once I returned to Europe, to my factory on Como Lake, all I could think of was: how can I go back to America? Well . . . I succeeded".

After the wedding and the honeymoon, Egon took the plane to New York. Diane decided to take the boat. "I wanted to arrive there slowly, taking the time to think about my life, to plan my future", says Diane in an amused voice, hinting at how independent and non-conformist she was already back then. "I was so nauseous because of the pregnancy that I didn't do much thinking on the boat", she adds while laughing. "But of one thing I was sure: I wanted to be an independent woman, who could live a man's life in a woman's body".

Diane's tone becomes more reflective, as she continues sharing her life story: "At that point, I didn't yet know what I wanted to do. What I did know was what type of woman I wanted to be . . . You know", she adds, "there are many doors in front of you when you start your life. The door that gets you going is not necessarily the most glamourous one. But it's a starting point, and I started with what was around me: the scarf printing place in Italy, which I leveraged to invent my life. With a small child at home, I travelled between the US and Italy to produce sample dresses in the factory in Italy and tried selling them in America. In the beginning, I had miserable orders: 15, 30, 55 dresses. But slowly, sample dresses became a collection, a skirt and a top became a dress, and this one dress became the iconic wrap dress". Diane stops for a few seconds, and then in a nostalgic tone, adds, "People always say that I invented the wrap dress, but it's the wrap dress that invented me, also if it took a long time for me to realise that. My initial unglamorous door, the factory of Angelo Ferretti on Lake Como, helped me make my dream of independence come true".

Diane's wrap dress turns 50 in 2024. And, for this special occasion, the Fashion & Lace Museum in Brussels has launched an exhibition dedicated to the wrap dress: "Women Before Fashion". An exhibition I visited in spring 2023, right after meeting Diane in person for the first time, following her opening speech in Brussels' town hall. An exhibition in which I continued to breathe her energy: colours, patterns, boldness, creativity, strength, femininity, seduction—all reunited in the declinations of this iconic dress.

"I always wanted to make dresses from woman to woman, that's why the exhibition is called 'Women Before Fashion': to me, women always came before fashion. By wearing these little dresses, women felt good. And when you feel good, you look good, and become confident. As I was selling these dresses to women, travelling throughout the US to expand my client base, I could see this collective confidence growing, which, in turn, boosted my confidence, to keep building DVF—my business—and Diane—myself, making me live the American dream!"

If you google DVF, you will find pictures of Diane with all the iconic people you can imagine. From the fashion world to the political one, from singers to artists. She was in the midst of it all. Her wrap dress quickly also became a symbol of freedom and independence for women, a trademark of the feminist movement. "Very few people knew it back then", admits Diane "but I called my first dress 'Angela', in honour of Angela Davis (one of the icons of the feminist movement in the US) after she had been imprisoned. In my own way, I was standing with her. I have always been a sure and proud feminist".

As a sign of her feminism, Diane also gave up her title of "Princess", which she had acquired by marrying Egon von Furstenberg. "When Gloria Steinem popularised the term 'Ms' [which was first put forward by Sheila Michaels in 1961] as a title for women, replacing the terms defining us in relation to a man, such as 'Mrs', I decided to swap my 'Princess' title to 'Ms'. I always wanted to be a 'Ms', not a 'Princess'".

Fifty years have passed since the invention of the term "Ms" and since the creation of DVF's brand, and the wrap dress remains just as iconic, worn by the types of Michelle Obama, JLo, Oprah Winfrey. Though what can seem like an indisputable success has a more nuanced story behind it—as it usually turns out to be. Diane's American dream was far from being, as we say in Italian, rose e fiori (i.e. sunshine and roses): the dress went up and down, fashionable, then forgotten, then rediscovered and relaunched; and Diane's company and life followed the same trajectory.

"At 27 I got separated, with two small kids and a huge company to run. A company which I kept very personal, and because of that went through ups and downs . . . It had a huge peak, in the 1970s and early 1980s, making my life adventurous and exhilarating. But by the mid-1980s, it was on the verge of bankruptcy. At that point, I was in my 40s: my children went off to boarding school, then college; I sold my business and stepped away from the fashion world; I got into an unhealthy relationship with a man—who wanted me to be quiet, small—and got lost in that; I started to question my style, myself; I lost my voice and—I am convinced because of that—had tongue cancer. My 40s were a difficult period, a period from which though I managed to get back up. By redesigning myself once more: I rebuilt my business, married my long-time love and lover—to whom I am still married today, became a grandmother, started living a healthier life—accelerated by this face-to-face experience with cancer. And by doing all of these things, by following what make me happy and healthy, I became successful again".

SUCCESS IS A FAÇADE; AUTHENTICITY IS THE REAL DEAL

Diane's eyes show resilience as she explains how she got back up. "I want to share, though, my take on success with you: making it, selling it . . . it's a game. The reality is different. When I was at my peak, when people thought I was at my highest success point ever, I knew it wasn't true because inside me I had issues. While when they thought I was over, that I had failed, I knew it was not the case either because I still had strength in me. Success is always relative. And failure is a natural and necessary part to it. Not only that; it is a part which has the power to transform you".

Failure is often a closing door. "Another one opens", says Diane. "You change the way you go and discover a direction which would have never been there without this failure". Diane always likes to remind people that life is a journey: the weather changes, the landscape changes, the circumstances change. It takes twists and turns, and failures and successes are what make our life interesting. "I am lucky to have lived a very full life, to feel fulfilled, and I always say I should be 350 years old with everything I have gone through—with intensity, with passion, without fear".

"So my business has been that: a mix of failure and success. I heard my son saying recently in an interview that for them, my business was like a third sibling. The one that goes in and out of rehab: sometimes it makes them proud, sometimes it's on the verge of suicide", Diane laughs loudly as she repeats her son's words. "But that's why if we want to talk about leadership, I am not sure I am a good leader".

Without realising it, my face shows my surprise: to me she is a leader, in so many ways. Diane looks at me and takes a short moment of reflection, and then reacts to my surprised expression. "Actually, let me correct that, I am a leader: if you inspire, you lead, and I am always amazed at the amount of people that felt their lives were affected by my words, my example, my support. Let's correct that", she says as to affirm it to herself. "I should recognise I am a leader; I am not though the most consistent manager in terms of my company's performance", she concludes. "The one advice I feel I should share when it comes to leadership is that weather you are a person, you have a brand, or run a company, the closer and truer you are to yourself, the better you are at what you do, and the freer you are in your job, in your life. Build complicity with yourself, wink at yourself in the mirror, and when you go to sleep at night, be glad that you are you. Yourself, your character, is the only thing you have complete control of, so that's where your focus should be".

Diane and I speak about this feeling of control over our lives, which she calls "being *in charge*". "I remember the first time I really felt *in charge*: my mother put me alone on a train from Brussels to Paris. I must have been eight or nine. I was a little scared, but I made sure not to show it. And that is true every time you feel *in charge*: there is a part of you that feels scared, uncomfortable, overwhelmed, but the excitement of being *in charge* overcomes the fear", as she says these words, I still perceive the excitement of this feeling in her voice. "Being *in charge* is first and foremost a commitment to ourselves: we own our imperfections and they become our assets, we own our vulnerabilities and they become our strength. It's not aggressive, but it's powerful. The women in charge are the women I think of when designing".

I ask Diane to share some advice with me, with those who will be reading these words, on how to build and maintain this commitment to ourselves over time. She shares a perfectly structured path to it. "Being in charge has four core elements. First, it means to *connect*: each of us has a magic wound, capable of creating connections. I try every day to connect one person I know with one person they would have otherwise not met. Second, it means to *expand our horizons*: once per week, give quality time to someone you would typically not give attention to. That expands your horizons, and it is magic.

Third, it means to *inspire*: to me, the best way is storytelling, like what I am doing now. Remembering that it's not your successes but your challenges and vulnerabilities that will speak to others. And fourth, *advocate*: find a cause, something you care about, and go for it, fight for it—no matter what. Doing these four things, will make you feel in charge and, more importantly, it will make you feel good about yourself".

As Diane says these words, I see a twinkle in her eyes. Her pragmatism and realism though quickly take over: "It doesn't mean being perfect or always feeling like you are *in charge*. Believe me, I sometimes wake up and feel like a loser", she admits with strength in her eyes. "But only losers don't feel like losers", Diane adds while winking at me. "As we go through life, it is crucial to remember that there are many elements over which we don't have control or which we will inevitably lose to. You can't control your destiny: you can witness it and ride it as best as you can. And in your lifetime, you can lose your job, your family, your house, your wealth, your health—I lost most of them at some point. But the one thing you never lose is your character. And it's your character that will give you the strength to deal with losses and to redesign yourself. I am still redesigning myself at age 76, it truly never ends. This is why it's so, so important that you build that, your sense of self, as a starting point to lead your life and lead others", she says while slowing down—to somehow mark how important that has been for her.

DESIGN YOUR LIFE

"I was once in Sicily", Diane says with the tone of someone who is about to tell a story. "*Che bella la Sicilia* [how beautiful!]", she adds in Italian, as I smile back thinking I'll be there in just a couple of weeks for a sunny wedding—happily leaving rainy Brussels behind. "Well, I was thinking about this idea of redesigning my life, and because I was in Sicily, I drew a Greek temple on a piece of paper. On the top I wrote 'redesign your life', and then I started building the columns below. The first is your *character*. This sense of self we were just speaking about. You should be your refuge and your shelter, and all other relations should be a plus, not a must. The second is our *body*, and our *brain*. I mean it's just crazy what we can do with it: exercise it, modify its shape. There is so much power within our bodies. To not speak about our brain: it's this incredible machine we have in our heads, which we don't even know how it works, but it makes us do amazing things—and we must take care of it. The third column is our *heart*. To me, our heart means being human, caring for others, being empathic—I hope this is the next trait we'll start seeing as strength, as an asset for leadership, instead of all the self-interest dominating our world. And I am convinced that only by being humans in the true sense, we will save humanity. The fourth, is our *purpose*. What we do at work, how we use our time, our sense of expression towards the outside world. And the fifth is what I do with my job: *aesthetics*. What you wear, what you surround yourself with, the power of colour. I did this nice drawing of this Greek temple, with all my key words to redesign our lives, and, once back home, I proudly showed it to my grandson, who said: 'grandma, you forgot nature'. He was totally right, nature is such a source of inspiration for me, so I added *nature*. I like odd numbers though, so I decided to add a 7th column: *rituals*. We do so many things in our life, every single day of our life, without even thinking about it. Going to bed, eating, taking a bath. All these are simple things, but these rituals are a core part of our inner strength and our capacity to redesign our life".

As Diane is concluding the sentence, with an accomplished look in her eyes, she suddenly changes tone and starts speaking again, "For the rest, you must just do your best: go with the river, never swim against the current. Adapt, pay attention to others, connect with people, expand your horizons, inspire others, and get inspired—I find my inspiration in nature and in women. But, above all, always stay true to yourself. That sets you free: even if you are in jail, even if you are under torture, you will be free if you stayed true to yourself. And yes, it can get lonely, especially when you are at the top, but it is the most important thing of all".

I am impressed by how Diane has clearly defined some key concepts in her life: being *in charge, designing your life*. She is a creative mind uniquely combined with order, definition and structure.

Without going into details, I share with Diane that I have been feeling a little lost over the past days and hours in dealing with something that was happening at work. Of course, I am lucky to have my friends and my partner who is always there to listen and support, but I felt confused by external advice, with how I felt, and a little tired of dealing with the backlash that you often get when you are a strong woman, especially when your strength, your confidence, your drive, threatens the "strength" of insecure men. I am about to ask her how she dealt with such moments in her career, and what her advice is, but without me needing to be explicit, Diane jumps straight in. "I don't really go to my friends to ask for advice", she states without hesitation. "I listen to others, but then I go to myself—I listen to my heart". We both stay in silence for a moment, as I realise that I tend to do the same: I trust my gut, my advice, my internal voice. But it also makes it feel lonelier—as if, finally, what we really always have is (only) ourselves.

"You remember what my mother taught me?", says Diane. "Fear is not an option, and no matter what, never be a victim. That is the best advice I ever received, because it means you have control over your life, you can trust yourself, be true to yourself, and just keep going ahead—no matter what happens . . . What zodiac sign are you?", she asks in a curious voice, as if for a moment our roles have been switched. "Leo, ascendant Leo"—I respond with a curious smile, as I am neither an expert nor a believer in signs but, somehow, I often get asked that question. "Interesting. . .", says Diane, "I can see you are strong and ambitious. What do you want to achieve in your lifetime?", she asks again. "I want to fix what is wrong and do it while being in charge—maybe one day I'll get to be the prime minister of my country or lead an even bigger organisation", I respond with a mix of conviction and shyness in my voice. As ambitious as I am, I always struggle to state my dreams, fearing a mix of two things: I might be setting myself up for failure if I say it out loud, and I might be perceived as threatening by others if they perceive my drive and ambition. But Diane has none of that: "Go for it, go for it, go for it", she says repeatedly with all her conviction. "You only regret the things you don't do, and mistakes just open doors. You know?", her voice becomes sweeter, maternal, and encouraging—as she clearly perceives I am seeking reassurance: "Sometimes, you feel lonely on your horse, it's true. But at least you have a horse, and a flag, and if there is no army behind yet, there will be one day. The important thing is that you are on that horse and that you know where you want to go. Clarity is everything!" As she says these words, Diane and I exchange a moment of complicity, before switching back to our roles. I re-take the lead on asking questions, she on responding, and we continue our interview.

A CHAOTIC WORLD, IN NEED OF WOMEN'S SOLUTIONS

Speaking of horses and flags, I ask Diane what her take is on the world we live in today, filled with divisive flags and competing horses. "We live in such a chaotic world, so chaotic", she says shaking her head. "The entire world is changing, and no one knows where we are going. And the way we define things . . . I mean, everything is so confusing. It seems as if truth has no value. And truth with no value is the most depressing thing you can imagine". I hear the depression in her voice.

Over the years, Diane's career and focus have expanded. Of course, she's an iconic designer, which dress made millions of women feel beautiful and confident, but her designs are first and foremost a means to an end: empowering women. This is why, over the years, Diane transformed into a philanthropist and into a leader beyond the fashion industry, using her voice, her time and her influence to bring change in our world. Among others, she's launched the DVF awards, supporting each year five women who have demonstrated leadership, strength, and courage in their commitment to women's causes.

"With age, I realise that this has become the most important part of my job, of my life. Doing things that help others, lifting women up. I also like helping men, don't get me wrong", she adds with a cheeky smile. "I love men. And being a feminist is not at all about hating men, it's simply about creating equality. But as a group, I am drawn to women—because I think women bring solutions and that us women could be the answer to many of the problems our chaotic world is facing today".

In a reflective tone, Diane goes on sharing her take on women: "I know how much strength women have within them . . . We often hide it, because of what society tells us: it is men, not women, who should appear strong. But that is bullshit, even for the most submissive woman: the moment there is a problem in the house, you can be certain the woman will be the one standing up. If there is a fire, she will find a solution to save everyone. What I wish to see is this: that every woman could feel that strength and own it, not only when there is a fire or an emergency in the house, but every single day of her life. And helping one woman, two women, thousands of women, find that strength is the most fulfilling thing I can do".

As she says these words, I think back to the opening of the DVF exhibition in Brussels, just a few weeks before this online interview we had planned for the book.

I am the first to arrive—my Dutch dad raised me with the anxiety of being late—in this majestic room of the Brussels townhall: dark wooden walls, a red moquette with noble patterns. I wonder if I am in the right place but, as I am approaching one of the municipality staff to ask, I start seeing women entering the room. Teenagers and "lived women" (as Diane likes calling herself, "How long have you lived?" should replace "How old are you?" according to Diane's philosophy of life), business women, journalists, fashion aficionadas. All in their DVF outfits: long dresses, midi dresses, skirts, jumpsuits, jackets. I gather I am in the right place, as the whole room fills up within minutes with this army of colourful and confident women: a homage to Diane's life, a testament of Diane's impact.

I sit in the first rows and, while waiting for Diane to arrive, the ladies around me start chatting, recalling anecdotes of their first DVF dress, of how that made them feel. "I bought it in the early 2000s, as a gift to myself on a bad day". "This dress was by mum's. I remember looking at her as she would get ready, put make-up on, slip into this dress, dreaming to have one of my own one day". I hear them speak of their jobs, and figure most of them occupy roles of responsibility—telling myself they are the women *in charge* which Diane was referring to, the women bringing the solutions and the leadership our chaotic world needs. It's as if I have entered this special DVF world, made of bold, chatty, ambitious and supportive women—waiting for their muse to arrive. I look around once more, in search of signs of Diane's arrival, and notice this beautiful but austere room had transformed within minutes into a bubbly space, filled with patterns and colours. A room filled with women living and leading in their own way.

LIFE AS A CONDUIT

As I continue looking around myself, in this large wooden room, I see, from far, Diane's hair, her iconic silhouette, portrayed over the years even by Andy Warhol, entering the main door. A warm applause fills the room as she walks down the aisle. Diane waves, smiles, advancing confidently and graciously in a green and black flowery dress, matching her wavy brown hair and bright dark eyes. As she reaches the front, she immediately undoes the set-up that had been prepared for her and the moderator: two chairs behind a formal table. She pulls the table back, moves the chairs to the front, so that everybody can see them. Her staff on the side wonder if they should do something, but she is fully in charge and, once happy with the new set-up, Diane sits down—ready to talk to us all, hoping that this moment can help the women in the room celebrate or rediscover their inner strength and confidence.

"My life is my life, of course", says Diane to us women eagerly waiting to hear her speak, "but in the end, my life is also a conduit. I am now at the sunset of it, and it is no longer so much about me, rather about the corridor I lead, for other people to find themselves and shine. And the best satisfaction I can ask for is hearing that I encouraged people to be themselves, is seeing a room like this one filled with women who gained confidence—be it through my words or through my little wrap dress. And I know, in my heart, that you ladies sitting here, and women everywhere, if given the space, the voice, the opportunities, can bring the solutions we need to fix our global problems—and can lead us out of this mess, becoming a conduit for the generations to come".

During our online interview, I follow-up on this opening statement from our meeting in Brussels to better understand, according to Diane, a true leader, how "capable of acting as a conduit" looks like. "To me, the real badass women, the true leaders, are the ones who get things done, who create solutions in families, in communities, in organisations. Not necessarily, or not only, the ones who are all the way at the top. And this is why I recognise and try and lift up those types of women and leaders through the DVF awards", she explains with pride in her smile. "It is true" she continues as she is still thinking about these leaders, "we do live in a chaotic and sometimes scary world, but it is also true that there are networks of people who do good work. People who do care about civilisation, about having healthy people and a healthy planet. Who don't work for the purpose of money, but for the purpose of having an impact—similar to you, Gaia", she says. "So, to me, what is important today is to link these people, these leaders, to create a mattress in the middle of high and lows, of left and right wings, amplifying the work and the impact that they can have on our planet. We do have to believe in the light, and cherish the light, and increase the light, because eventually it's this light that will put the darkness away", says Diane with her unique optimism and wisdom.

"I am not naïve though", she adds right after. "Our political leaders, those who hold the actual power are often disappoin-ting. It is because they are tied with politics, with short-term interests. And unfortunately, even if leadership should be about inspiring, about doing good, lifting others up, the reality is that too many of those we call 'leaders' think about them-selves, not about others; are caught into a cycle of greed and auto-referential egoism. Maybe", says Diane with a doubtful tone—which is untypical of her—"maybe it's the whole con-cept of leadership that should disappear. Making and creating communities of people who can decide together would be better. I mean I don't know", she adds while gesturing with her hand to move away from the topic as she struggles to artic-ulate a certain and conclusive thought on it. "But something is wrong, and we do need a rethink. Of that, I am sure. And in the meantime, I will continue inspiring and putting that inspiration at scale, serving as a conduit, hoping it can already make a small difference in today's world".

THEN AND NOW

We discuss the years in which Diane started her career, the boomer's generation, the age of opportunities, of consum-erism. And how the situation is different for my generation, the millennials, as well as for GenZ, in terms of the world we live in, the problems we need to fix, and the type of experi-ence we have as we design ourselves and our careers in this uncertain world.

"I was lucky in my career because I became my own boss. I didn't have to put up with being treated as a piece of meat at work, which was the case for most women in the 1970s, 1980s. The average man thought women were there at their disposal, and I was in the position of saying 'no', of not depending on these dynamics to move forward in my career". The feminist movement, which accompanied Diane throughout her life, played a huge part in shifting the role of women, at home and at work. And Diane, as her own boss, as a CEO, as a woman *in charge*, was a precursor of many of these changes. The reality, though, is that still today parity is far from being reached, and still today Diane and her approach to work and to life can be considered forward-looking, *avant-garde*, for women and for men.

Diane nods in response to my statement. "The MeToo and TIME's UP movements we saw recently were so crucial, but also telling of a deep truth: still too many men treat women as pieces of meat, even in 2023", she explains. "And this battle for parity, for respect, is far from being over. Luckily there are amazing women leaders emerging, designing new types of companies, of work cultures, setting an example of how things can and should be done differently".

With enthusiasm in her voice, Diane tells me that she loves this new generation of leaders. "Meeting young entrepreneurs helped me realise that younger generations have a new way of doing things, and we all need to evolve in this direction. They are breaking the rules we had built decades ago, by taking the middleman out, by going straight to the point, using mathematical formulas and all sorts of innovative methods to simplify and improve our life. At the same time, it's a generation that needs to deal with an increased number of complex global challenges. This is the reason

I often tell young entrepreneurs: why not leverage this capacity to innovate and to simplify things and apply it to do good? To fix the big problems we have in this world—be it migration, climate change, inequalities. I would love to see more of that . . .", states Diane with this wisdom she carries in every word. "Of course, I can't know, but I sometimes wonder if I wouldn't try to do that—if I were 25 today. I love breaking rules, I love finding solutions, and I think our world needs smart and fearless people advancing the global good, for the sake of humanity and our planet".

Diane took a different path back then, at age 25. "I chose design as my path. Or maybe I didn't choose it so explicitly, but it became my path. A creative path which is, though, different from art because it requires you to deal with pragmatism, while still selling a dream. And because it gives you an entry point into the daily lives of people around you, by bringing something useful, usable, and not only a beautiful object to admire". A path which, luckily for us, she still leveraged to positively influence the world. "This means that through design and fashion, you impact daily habits, daily decisions, you shape how people feel and act—and you can and should use this closeness and intimacy with people's life also to bring some positive change. I tried to do just that".

SEDUCTION, THE POWER OF WOMEN

A designer, a philanthropist. A role model to women, a muse for artists. Across her multiple hats and across the multiple phases and twists of her career, there is one additional trait which has served Diane well, and on which she shares her reflections: seduction.

"I always knew I was seductive", she admits, "but never thought I was beautiful. I am grateful for that. Beauty fades and, for women who rely only on their beauty, getting older can be hard. I feel as if every wrinkle, every mark on my face is a testament. Of my life, of my travels, of the Sun, of the air, of the smiles, of the tears. They tell my story; they show how fully I lived. But this is not how most women feel, especially in the fashion world and especially at my age. For those who centred their identity and life around their beauty, time can be harsh. As they get older, they feel invisible, as if they have lost a battle, as if they have been defeated. And I always found that sad, because the final part of your life is when you should feel fulfilled, not defeated".

"This is why seduction to me is different from beauty", Diane adds with an explanatory tone. "And this is why, when I say seductive, I don't mean only the physical part. To me seduction is something we have and bring as women, just as we bring solutions. Seduction is our capacity to make the solution happen, to persuade others that our solution—the one we think is the best—is the best also for them. This is why intelligence and seduction are a great match: you need the intelligence to find the solution, and the seduction to make it happen".

Reacting to her words, I share an anecdote from a class discussion I had a few years back, touching on this exact point. During a Harvard leadership course, a guy asked how (pretty) women in the class managed the relation between intelligence and seduction. After an initial awkward silence, as no woman wanted to speak up and "auto-define" herself as pretty, a Dutch girl started speaking. And then I took over. We gave a similar response to what Diane shared: they are linked, and it's normal that each of us uses our way of being, of behaving, our strengths, to bring people along in the direction we want them to go. Of course, with clear red lines, but it's impossible to just separate the two. It's like asking someone how he or she would use their intelligence in a different body, or with a different character. And we also shared with our classmates that, to us, "pretty" was not the bottom line: it was the overall way of being for certain women, their charisma—which goes beyond the merely physical aspect.

The reaction we got was unexpectedly harsh, mainly from women. Accusing us of using our charm, our looks, our smile, to navigate and get ahead compared to other (less pretty, or "seductive") women.

"Oh, that's jealousy", says Diane with a dismissive tone. "If there is jealousy, I just don't pay attention to that. It is something I don't feel, and on which I don't want to use my energies". She stops speaking, and I feel admiration for how clear-cut and easy-going she is on the topic—as I tend to do the opposite: overthink these types of situations and feel deeply hurt when someone tries to undermine me because of jealousy, or because they feel threatened, not because of something I have actually done or said, because of something I have control of.

"Well . . ." continues Diane, understanding I am looking for advice. "If I see someone could potentially be or become jealous, my tendency is to seduce them. By sharing my vulnerability, my insecurity. This allows them to relate to me, to you, and to stop seeing us necessarily as competitors, because we look better, or have a better job, or more convincing ideas, or whatever it is. When people feel threatened by you, you have to be compassionate, more compassionate than them, and you'll manage to invert the situation. But also", she adds with a witty look in her eyes, "when you have that moment, enjoy it. Take it as a compliment".

We both laugh out loud.

"When I was very young", continues Diane, still smiling, "I was on the first page cover of *The Wall Street Journal* (WSJ). On that day, I was travelling by plane, and I boarded with a pile of newspapers in my hands—and on the top of the pile was the WSJ. I remember it was only men in the plane. I arrived in my pretty dress, showing my legs, and sat in my seat. The guy next to me turned around and asked why a pretty girl like me was reading the WSJ. I looked at him and thought, 'What an idiot'. I could have turned around and told him I was being featured. But I didn't say anything. I go back to the complicity one has with oneself: you don't always need to react and tell people things. When something bad happens to you, when someone is jealous, or underestimates you, or undermines you, you can always decide to store it, and just think, 'When I tell my story, when I write my book, when I do my Ted talk, this will be my best anecdote'".

As I am looking at my notes to move to the next question, Diane starts speaking again: "Actually, I have one last trick that might come in handy to you or to women, or men, reading this. When you are being interviewed, or are trying to sell something to someone but are worried they might have something against you, ask yourself exactly that: 'what is the one thing they could have against me?' And then bring it up first: it's the best way to neutralise it. So you see?", she says in a pragmatic and relaxed tone. "There are so many things you can do to manage backlash, jealousy, by using your seduction power in different ways. But my advice: just be proud of having such power, and don't pay attention, don't waste time on these type of things, or people, that are just trying to undermine you. It will save you a lot of energy and headaches".

JUST BE YOU

Whenever Diane speaks, shares her story, her advice, there are two things that impress me: her capacity to make everything sound relative—which probably comes also with the wisdom of age—and to carry a sense of liberation, of being free from restrictions, from judgements, from constraints; coupled with her parallel capacity to believe and stand by everything she says and sees. It's as if she relativises things, but without becoming distant or detached from them, remaining rooted in life and in all its dynamics. To me, this duplicity makes her voice even more special.

"I grew up with the feminist movement", explains Diane, "with the movement behind our liberation. I carry its flame in everything I do, in everything I say, because I want every woman to feel that lightness. So my final words are: don't be afraid to be you, because you are your asset, with all your strengths and vulnerabilities—and it's being true to yourself that will make you shine in the long run, not your capacity to adhere or fit to outside expectations or standards. And, more importantly, it's being true to yourself that will make you happy to be you when you go to bed at night".

As we say goodbye, Diane invites me to join her for the DVF awards in Venice—and I, of course, accept, already imagining this dreamy night filled with inspiration and impressive badass women from all over the world.

As I press the "leave meeting" button, I feel emotional, energised, empowered—and very excited about seeing Diane soon again in Venice.

I leave with a re-found clarity. To relativise what is happening at work, to not allow myself or others to put me in the victim role, and to take things in my hands: following my advice, being true to myself.

"Authenticity"—one word which Diane loves and never gets tired of repeating—holds the power to guide me and many of us through the twists and turns of life. Reminding us of the inner strength we all bring, inspiring us to be *in charge* and to lead, and enabling us to redesign our lives, every single day, by simply being ourselves.

As I finish this chapter, I think of deleting and rewriting the introduction. I don't like it. I don't like seeing myself in a passive and frustrated role, because that's rarely who I am and surely not who I want to be. And the call with Diane was sufficient to get me back on my feet, in my active and *in charge* mode.

"Leaving our emotions aside is something we sometimes do when going through difficult moments", Diane had shared with me as a final piece of advice. "Something we do, though, for our own sake, to give us the head space to focus, not for the sake of others". By listening to her advice, and making it mine, I didn't end up sharing my frustrations at work, because it wasn't strategic in order to steer things in the direction I wanted to—towards making sure we could all recreate a positive dynamic, refocus on work and no longer on personal power struggles.

But after deleting, rewriting, deleting the introduction again, I decided to stand by its original version and share these feelings with you all. Because these moments happen, especially to women in charge. And because—as Diane says—it's important to share our challenges, not only our successes. As I reinclude the original introduction, Diane's words resonate in the back of my head: "I go back to the complicity one has with oneself: you don't always need to react and tell people things. You can also store it and when something bad happens to you, when someone is jealous, or underestimates you, or undermines you, just think, 'When I tell my story, when I write my book, when I do my Ted talk, this will be my best anecdote'".

Here is my book, here is my anecdote, here are my doubts and my feelings—a part of the twists and turns in the everyday life of an authentic woman *in charge*.

• 5 •

FREEDOM
Tawakkol Karman

ONCE UPON A TIME, in what is today known as Yemen, lived a queen. Her name was Bilqis, and she was the Queen of Sheba.

The *Bible*, the Aramaic *Targum Sheni*, the *Quran*, the Ethiopian *Kebra Negast*—all narrate her story. The Queen of Sheba, also known as the "Queen of the South", ruled her land in peace and prosperity, worshipping the Sun. One day though, she learned about King Solomon, of his boundless wisdom and close bond with God. As a seeker of truth, she decided to travel from Arabia to Jerusalem on a camel, to meet this wise King. She carried caravans of spices, precious stones, and gold as a gift for Solomon. Upon meeting him, the Queen tested his wisdom and connection with God through a series of riddles. Convinced by the King's knowledge, Bilqis, the Queen of Sheba, decided to convert to Solomon's God—bringing her people into a new era, the era of monotheism.

Her legend occupies thousands of pages, hundreds of movies, millions of evening stories—sitting around the fireplace or the dinner table. Truth is, though, that this Queen has done much more than inspire mythological tales. She inspires, still today, Yemeni women to lead. To demand respect and to fearlessly play their role in society. "If the Queen of Sheba did it thousands of years ago, why shouldn't a Yemeni woman, like me, be able to do so today?", says Tawakkol in an authoritative voice. The Queen of Sheba is the proof that today's Middle East is far from being what it used to be: a region in which women could rule, in which female rulers brought peace and prosperity, and in which men looked up to queens and to women as leaders, just as they did to kings and to men—in full syntony with religious beliefs.

"Even as a child I felt inspired by the Queen of Sheba. She was a strong and wise woman, from my country and my culture. I believe in her story, and thanks to her, I believe in the ability of Yemeni people to respect women", continues Tawakkol—as I catch a look of admiration for this Queen in her dark brown eyes. "They are so proud of our Queen, you see the respect in how they speak about her, in how their eyes shimmer when they mention her name. This gives me faith in myself as a Yemeni woman, and it gives me a deep conviction that the marginalisation of women in today's society is not in the blood, in the DNA, of Yemeni men. And for sure, it's against the DNA of Yemeni women", she adds with a complicit smile.

As we all sit comfortably on our sofas reading Tawakkol's courageous words, Yemen is in the midst of a complex war and an alarming humanitarian crisis. It's the poorest country of the Arab state region and over 75% of its population needs urgent humanitarian assistance, as of 2022. This means 30 million people suffering from hunger, lacking the most essential resources and services—from water to healthcare, from education to jobs. A total of 4 million have even been forced to leave their homes due to conflict.

And all of this has further exacerbated pre-existing gender inequalities: in 2017, Yemen was ranked by the World Economic Forum as the last country out of 144 countries in terms of gender equality—it couldn't get worse. Women have extremely low rates of participation in the public sphere, in paid work, in schools. As explained by UN Women, discrimination against them is ingrained in formal and informal justice systems and data still shows today record-high rates of violence against women—including forced and early marriage. Structural inequalities make it hard for women to emerge, but nothing is ever impossible. Tawakkol Karman is the proof of it.

JUST AS CAPABLE: EQUALITY IN A
CONSERVATIVE COUNTRY

She was born in the northern part of Yemen, in the late 1970s, as one of 10 siblings in her large family. Tawakkol's father, a lawyer and a politician, served but later resigned as a minister in the government of Ali Abdullah Saleh—the dictator who ruled Yemen from its unification in 1990 until 2012, the year in which he left power following the Yemeni Revolution. She studied commerce and political science in Yemen and started a career as a journalist, to then become an activist, a politician, and the *Mother of the Revolution* which led to the fall of the regime.

"My life, my path have been heavily influenced by the education I received as a child. I grew up in Taiz—that might not say much to you, but if you google it you'll read that it's a 'place of learning in a conservative country'—and that's exactly what it was. My sisters and I were taught by our mother and father that *we* were the ones who should bring change. That we shouldn't ask people to help us, but rather put ourselves in a position from which we can help others. That we shouldn't just ask questions, but search for answers. That we should be the ones on the frontlines, and not put the weight of responsibility on the others' shoulders, especially not on men's—starting from my three brothers. 'You should be outside the house with your brothers; you are just as capable of solving problems, of standing up for yourselves as boys are; you must carry your own responsibility for change', my father used to tell us girls over and over again", says Tawakkol with a proud look on her face. "This is how I became the woman I am. Convinced that I have all the power I need to bring change and that if I don't carry the responsibility and the force for change myself, I am just putting it on other peoples' shoulders, asking them to bring the change I want to see. And that's not fair, or at least that's simply not me", she adds.

"Because of this upbringing, to me it was the most natural thing to act whenever I wanted to see change—even if the cultural and religious norms surrounding me stated I shouldn't. In school, I became the president of the student body, the spokesperson for students. I led a lot, believe me, a lot of demonstrations against the teachers and the dean", she says smiling, as if she is seeing images of a young Tawakkol demonstrating against teachers passing in front of her eyes. "And when I started my career, I already felt deep down it was never about being a journalist *per se*, writing articles. It was always about bringing change, using my words, my pen—which is stronger than a sword—as a way of fighting injustice, of affirming the truth. Supporting colleagues who were imprisoned, or going to prison myself was part of my duty as a journalist fighting for her job, for press freedom. Just like I did at school, I became member of a journalists' union, and then its president . . . my activist soul emerged in everything I did since the very early days".

THE IRON WOMAN

As she describes the first steps of her career, I can already see why she is referred to as the *iron woman*. She pushes right through, to the point, without using many words. She calls things how they are, standing up for what she believes in, and not accepting half measures. I perceive this iron layer around her, as someone who had to face harsh and complex circumstances to get where she is. An iron layer framed by the bright and flowery hijab she is wearing, by the serious and at the same time hopeful look in her eyes. And by her smile: it appears seldom, given the heaviness of her life story and work, but when it does, it feels sincere and reassuring.

Tawakkol quickly tucks a side of her hijab into place, and then continues speaking: "By being a journalist, I started discovering what was happening behind the scenes in my homeland. The attacks against human rights, the terrorism, the corruption, the extreme corruption", she says while gesturing with her hands. "All supported by Saleh—the dictator. And while denouncing this, I started seeing expression rights shrinking. The government put limitations on press freedom, on opinions. They started closing newspapers, banning websites, imprisoning journalists, even killing some intellectuals who weren't aligned with the regime's views. And I decided to act, and by acting, I automatically put myself on the frontline. In 2005, I created my own organisation, Women Journalists Without Chains. Through this organisation, we advocated for rights and freedom, produced reports on human rights abuses in Yemen, while providing media skills trainings to journalists to ensure they could become stronger and better in doing their job, and in facing the backlash from the regime".

"Founding my own organisation was an important turning point in my path. I put myself into an institutional role, from which I could act, organise things my way, and from which I could claim my identity as a leader, as Tawakkol. It really changed how I perceived myself and how others perceived me. This is why I always advise others—if they want to lead—to start their own project, their own foundation, newspaper, or party. It gives them the freedom to do what they believe in, and to do it their way. In my case, through my organisation, I prepared the revolution in Yemen—we thought we needed broader system change, and I wanted to lead it my way", she

says while explaining the origin of the uprising. "What happened is that the more I would dig into the situation in my
country, the more I felt outraged. An outrage that, with the
passing of time, gave me one certainty: the only thing, the only
solution to all this was to end the dictatorship, to stand against
it until it was dismantled. This is how I started standing up to
our dictator: protecting rights to expression, and by doing so,
protecting all human rights, advocating for democracy, helping
my country build the tools it needed to break the regime—once
and for all. In 2007, I started organising sit-in protests in Sanaa
[the capital of Yemen], to raise the stakes and accelerate change.
Keep in mind", she adds with pride in her voice, "that this was
years before the Arab Spring happened, and we were already
on the streets. Every week I would be there—sometimes with
few people, sometimes with many—to call for press freedom
and respect for human rights. Of course, this had a cost: I was
imprisoned several times, and if not me, it would be others—I
spent so many hours trying to get journalists and activists out
of prison. It was hard, but it was needed, and it prepared the
ground for the 2011 uprising in my country".

"You know Yemen?", she asks suddenly with a smile. I respond
I've never been there, but that I lived for years in the Middle
East working in humanitarian aid and that I heard stories from
my colleagues as the organisation I worked with was providing
aid in Yemen right at the end of the Revolution (2011/2012)
and then at the start of the civil war (2014). I heard stories,
I kept up to date with what happened, but had not experienced it first-hand. "I love my country so, so much", continues
Tawakkol in a more upbeat voice. "We have a great geographical
position, natural resources, a rich environment, we have a history to be proud of, and most of all we have amazing people—
with so much potential! I know it deserves better than what

we have lived through over the past decades. I know in my heart that we have a great chance to be free, from tyranny, from corruption, from extremism. And a chance to be prosperous, without any dependence on others. There is no reason anything could stop us from getting there, if not for the lack of good governance we have been having for decades under this dictator. So this is what I was trying to change: through my sit-ins, my protests, my organisation. I was acting—with many others—to help Yemen achieve its full potential. You must understand that the economic crisis, the social crisis, the security crisis we lived in were all details, as they were linked to him, to Saleh, and to his bad governance. Meaning that ending his rule was our only possibility to achieve our dreams. This was very clear in my mind, but you know", she adds with a nervous smile, "it's not easy to stand up against a dictator, and to convince others to follow you in this fight—especially as a woman in a conservative country".

I ask what the turning point was in her fight against the dictator. "The Arab Spring. When we saw the protests starting in Tunis, followed by the fall of the dictatorship, and then saw protests moving to Libya, to Egypt, we also found the hope and the courage to do just that: not only protest for our rights, but protest until we overturned the regime and became free. This is what we did in 2011: I spent nine months living in a tent on "Change Square" in our capital, with thousands of other people, calling on the end of the dictatorship. The square had been transformed into a sea of flags, banners, and tents where we would sleep. My children and my husband would come and support me, and they were the first ones to tell me I should stay on the square: I was fighting for their future, for them to grow up in a free Yemen. It took a lot of perseverance, but I knew I couldn't give up. And when I was imprisoned, and maltreated, for organising protests, people showed up for me, and for the movement. They gave me the conviction of not leaving the square—no matter what. To the extent that when I was in prison and the guards told me that they would let me out in exchange of a signed paper declaring I would no longer be involved in protests, I didn't think twice: I took myself back to the cell. And it was worth it, because we succeeded: on the 25 of February 2012, Saleh resigned, ending 22 years of dictatorship".

PERSEVERANCE, A PATH TO FREEDOM

In my own small way, I feel a perseverance similar to Tawak-kol's. I recognise this internal voice that tells me to continue pushing, to not be afraid despite the backlash, reassuring me that it's simply part of being a change-maker, a trailblazer, or—in the case of Tawakkol—a revolutionary. "When I started the revolution, I always reminded myself and others of the Queen of Sheba. Not because I am the Queen", she adds to clarify she is not a megalomanic, "but because there is a respect for her. And during the protests, I got the confirmation of what I always thought about my people: if you put yourself out as someone who is close to them, who leads them, they will not look at your gender, they will not fear that you are a woman. Of course, this doesn't mean you won't have obstacles as a woman. Obstacles are there, from society, from dictators, from religious people, I had to navigate many of them—especially during my first steps as a leader", she explains. "But once peo-ple understood I wouldn't give up, I would persist, they started gathering behind me, protecting me, putting me in the centre of the circle during community meetings. They just stopped seeing the limits of me being a woman, and started respecting me as a leader, as Tawakkol. And I found in their eyes the same respect they have for the queens of our past. Bilqis, our Queen who ruled the great kingdom of Sheba, inspired me to work with those people, with the confidence that the misogynous culture is not in their blood, and I was proven right".

Tawakkol comes back to the Queen of Sheba as her source of inspiration, and I ask her what or who else inspired her—especially in the hardest moments she faced, be it in prison or in lonely parts of her journey. "The peaceful method", she responds without hesitation, "I was inspired by Mahatma Gandhi, by Nelson Mandela, by Martin Luther King. I spent nights reading their books, learning from them how to respond to violence through non-violence. They gave me the ability to speak to others, to convince them to follow me in this revolution, and the courage I needed to make it all happen. And this is the meaning of real leadership for me: feeling responsible for others, becoming part of the solution, and taking initiative to solve the problem—especially when this means putting yourself on the frontline, just as Gandhi, Mandela, and King did. They faced fears, troubles, attacks, all while helping others to not be afraid of pushing ahead, empowering them to be the source of the change they want to see in this world. And I tried to do the same; this is the reason I see myself as a leader: every day I encourage other women, or young people like yourself—be it male or female—to think of themselves as leaders, and to act as one. I'll never get tired of repeating this: if you don't take the responsibility of change on your shoulders, you will put the burden on others to act in your place. But careful", she says pointing her finger towards me in a teacher-like way, "this doesn't mean you must be the boss. You can lead at any level: in your family, in your community, in your team. If you are bringing solutions and helping others to face change, then you are a leader—and I call on everybody reading these words to be one, because the world desperately needs stronger and better leadership".

Tawakkol and I start reflecting on the status of our world, thorned by wars, poverty, inequalities, and societal polarisation. And on how this is a consequence of leadership failures: "We have a great failure of leadership, and of the values driving leadership, when we talk of governmental leadership, of their policies and practices. But", Tawakkol says with a sense of urgency in her voice "if we talk about leadership at other levels, organisational leadership, leadership of communities, of families, of NGOs, I believe leadership has become stronger over the past decade: there are more struggles, more sacrifices being made. For freedom, for justice, for equality, for good governments. At this level, there is a stronger attachment to values compared to just a couple of decades ago. There are people willing to risk their lives for these values, and this must be said and recognised, we simply can't put all leaders in the same box".

We both nod, and I look down at my notes to move to the next question. Tawakkol leans towards me and before I start speaking, says, "But you are right", she adds, still caught in her line of thought, "at the government level, at the global governance order, there are steps backwards. When democratic governments restrict rights, when they give up on their core democratic values, we see democracy retreating. And once democracy starts to retreat internally, we see the start of internal crises: racism, discrimination, the rise of the far right—or of extremist parties more generally, be it on the right or on the left. We must state the facts: democracy is threatened all around the world, because democratic

governments failed to protect it within their borders".
And data confirms this: according to the Democracy Index
of the Economist Intelligence Unit, a third of the world's
population lives under authoritarian rule while only 8%
enjoys a full democracy, with a new low for global democracy
reached in 2021—also due to the COVID-19 restrictions.

"But there is more to it, to what happens within the US, within
Europe, within democratic countries", continues Tawakkol.
"On top of internal issues, these countries also failed to protect democracy and to act in accordance with its values at the
international level, towards the rest of the world. There are
so many examples of this over the past few years, especially
from my region—the Middle East", as Tawakkol says these
words, her eyes become more severe. "They didn't provide
the necessary support to us rising during the Arab Spring,
they didn't stop the dictator Bashar al-Assad from his crimes
in Syria, they didn't stop Putin from his crimes in Syria or
in Georgia—no wonder he felt safe to go ahead in Ukraine.
They didn't act to protect people and to protect democracy,
and when they did act, they were the first ones to use undem-
ocratic methods—like in Afghanistan or in Iraq, where they
tortured, lied to, and hurt people. Truth is that they either just
stand and watch or act but not in line with their values, and
that puts all of democracies at risk. Because when a leader or a
government that claims to stand for democracy doesn't stand
by those values, they lose legitimacy, they lose moral integrity,
they lose their capacity to affirm democratic values among
their citizens and abroad. These political and geopolitical
decisions, made by democracies over the past decades,
provoked a real crisis of democratic models and the conse-
quent rise of extremism—within democracies and beyond.

Billions of people are suffering from the consequences of this democratic fragility".

As Tawakkol says these words, I am reminded of my years working in the Middle East—of the Syria war, of the crisis in Iraq, or of the excruciating situation in Palestine. And of how I learned by being on the ground that what seemed like geopolitical decisions, or simply a small part of the daily news for so many people living in the Western world, transformed into life-changing implications for millions of people living in these countries—impacting their safety, their access to emergency aid, their capacity to have their most basic rights respected. And I am reminded so clearly of how Syrians or Iraqis would tell me they felt let down, abandoned, even rejected by democratic countries—just when they needed them the most. Instead of protection and a safe harbour to rebuild their lives, they found walls and border controls, instead of feeling supported in standing up for their rights, they felt forgotten and left alone in their struggle for freedom.

"Our governments have to be brave", says Tawakkol. "They must return to the values of democracy and human rights, and not give a chance to extremism and racism to flourish. They should stop making alliances with dictators around the world: it makes them weaker, less legitimate. And they must gather the camp of the democratic countries, of human rights and freedom fighters, they must pull all these energies together, and support each other. Because we have a battle ahead of us: between the camp of democracy and the camp of tyranny, between the camp of people who believe in respect for each other, in equality, and those who believe in their superiority. This is the most dangerous fight—and it's right ahead of us. So we must keep going, and be ready for what is coming next, holding tight to our dreams".

WHAT CAN YOU DO FOR YOUR COUNTRY?

"How do you hold tight to your dreams?", I ask out of curiosity. "Since I was a child, I asked myself what I could do for my country. Not what *people* can do, but what *I* can do with others. How can *I* be a person who won't be forgotten . . . did you ever think of that?" I do, often, and assume many others do. Driven by this simultaneously altruistic and egoistic desire of leaving a mark, of being remembered also once we'll be gone. "Well", says Tawakkol, "this is something that drives me. That question continues guiding me, helping me to hold tight to my dream of freedom. Because sooner or later, we will prevail, I am certain of it. We are the ones carrying noble values and time will be on my side, on your side. This is why I tell others not to give up. To not give into fear, frustration, or obstacles. To always believe in themselves. If you remain patient, if you hold onto your moral integrity, time will be on your side". Tawakkol's eyes brighten up, as I see her already imagining the day on which she and her country will be free.

Following the revolution—spearheaded by Tawakkol, for which she was awarded the 2011 Nobel Peace Prize—and the fall of the dictatorship in Yemen, things didn't go as planned—meaning peace and freedom are still far from being a common currency in her home country. "After the revolution, we started working straight away on a new constitution. And wrote a beautiful, forward-looking one: ingraining human rights, including the rights of women—guaranteeing a role for women within the new Yemeni society we wanted to build. But then the counter-revolution came, supported by regimes such as Saudi Arabia, the United Arab Emirates, and Iran. Truth is that these countries didn't want democracy to prevail: they didn't want to allow for a real participation and power-sharing among the people, they didn't want women to have rights, or even worse occupy leadership roles. They feared losing power, and even more feared women taking some of it. They worried that if Yemeni women would get rights following the uprising, then women within their countries would also revolt, and ask for rights . . . which is anyway what is happening today in Iran—where people are exhausted by the oppressive regime. I must admit", continues Tawakkol with a sad look in her eyes, "that this counter-revolution broke our dreams. It brought our country back to war, into chaos. But this doesn't mean we should stop fighting for it: the only way to fail is to stop our journey", she adds in a firm tone. "We must continue, continue and continue. We must not believe in people who lose hope, who are taken over by frustrations, who stop when faced with obstacles. We must remain on the frontlines, bringing hope and rejecting fear. And to the youth reading this, especially the ones living under authoritarian regimes, remember that you will be the leaders one day. Not all these old people, these old men, dominating our society and creating the chaos we are currently in. You will be. And you must believe in yourself, in the fact that you are and will be a leader, to change your communities and your countries, be it in Africa, in the US, or in Yemen—I have trust in the new generations to be the change our world needs", she adds with an encouraging smile.

I smile back and try and bring Tawakkol towards the topic of women and leadership, or better: the relation between leadership and power for women.

To me, it's indeed not a coincidence that the face of the revolution in Yemen, just like in other countries that went through the Arab Spring, or in many other revolutions from the past, is Tawakkol—a woman. Women are historically present in moments when society needs to change, providing the courage and the leadership for deep and disruptive change to happen. But once the revolution is over, when it comes to power, to authority, women are pushed back into their old roles and men reclaim the reins of countries and organisations. This has been the pattern also in the aftermath of the Arab Spring.

"I agree with you", says Tawakkol. "Women make great leaders in the transformation period, in revolutions. But when the situation becomes stable again, men hijack their power . . . how many times did we hear them say: 'no—you don't have the experience, you don't know how to govern, how these things work. It's a man's job'? Men just push us out. Aware of this pattern, we—the women that led the revolutions against the dictators in Yemen, Egypt, Tunisia, Libya—organised to prevent this from happening, ingraining all our rights within the constitutions. But the counter-revolution started, men ignored the change we brought, and stepped over our rights—yet again. And this is bad news, very bad news for the world. I'll tell you why", she says, clearing her voice. "I believe in female leadership as a key solution to today's madness. We have within us the nature of being mothers, of being incorruptible when it comes to the future of our children, when it comes to solving problems for the generations to come. If you look at the map of extremisms, women are rare, very rare. And we should be proud of this: as women, we did not create the chaos we live in today, we didn't fail our countries and our children, we didn't fall into extremism. That's exactly why we must put ourselves out there, to lead us out of this chaos. But to do so, we must take that power, grab those roles of authority, of decision-making in governments: because men will otherwise just use our power when they need change, to then hijack it again and preserve their authority and dominance on everybody else".

"I have something else to say on this", says Tawakkol, "a message for women: if you are a leader with no authority, with no actual power over things and over people, it means you play a decorative role. And this should never ever be the position of women: we should not accept any decorative role. If we do, we do a disservice to women and to society. We allow men to say, 'You see? You are in power', while continuing to actually hold the power themselves. Women must be outspoken about this: they must reject such roles, or at least be frank with themselves and with their people when they realise they have been put in such a decorative role, to then get out of it".

Tawakkol looks straight into my eyes, "Let's be honest", she says. "Most governments and companies put women in high-level positions to play a decorative role. For example, Tunisia right now has a woman prime minister. People who don't know the context, or who can't read between the lines, including many people from international organisations, think this is a great achievement—I heard them celebrating this as a success. But celebrating what?" says Tawakkol, in an upset tone. "Putting a woman in a fake leadership position, to be the shadow of the dictator? To me, she is not a leader, she is a doll. And women shouldn't accept that—this is just a different and more sophisticated way of continuing to exclude us from actual power".

TRUE POWER. IF NOT, WALK AWAY

I ask her which women hold real power, and she goes silent. After some thinking, Tawakkol speaks again. "Well, Aung San Suu Kyi in Myanmar. To me, she was a great leader: she faced the army, she made a strong opposition, and paid a stark price by being imprisoned. But when the army allowed her to become prime minister, in an ornamental role, not in a real power role, she lost her legitimacy as a leader and accepted to be downgraded to being ornamental. And paid heavy consequences for this choice. She lost the trust of people, of her citizens, of the international community, because she didn't stick to her values, because she didn't say the truth to her people, because she let a horrible genocide happen against the Rohingyas. For me, she should have never accepted this decorative role, which required compromising her own strength, her own power, her own values. My advice to women, before agreeing to taking on a high position, is to ensure they have real power, real authority—otherwise you shouldn't accept. The case of Aung San Suu Kyi is a clear reminder of this".

I jokingly say that this doesn't sound like an example of a woman who succeeded in holding real power, and Tawakkol goes back into thinking mode. "Well . . .", she continues in an unsure tone, "I can think of only women from the past. Margaret Thatcher was a model of real leadership. And Benazir Bhutto, of course! I always look up to her as a leader in a conservative society—similar to mine. It goes without saying that we can never know 100% what happened behind the scenes, but I consider them as role models, as women truly in charge. Nowadays, especially in my region, we don't have women like them: the few holding leadership positions are playing the game, taking on decorative roles to beautify the dictatorial system, while in reality activists are in jail, human rights are not respected, people are not free. It's a façade of progress in human and women's rights, not real progress—and we can't be proud of that!"

We start discussing the difficulties we face as women at different stages in our lives. Difficulties which—as explained by

Tawakkol—are amplified for those living in countries where Islam (or religion more broadly) is used as a reason, a justification, a weapon to exclude them from society, to hold them back from power. A situation that has further deteriorated in some contexts following protests and uprisings, with a backlash targeting women activists and civil society members—to silence their voice. Women in Afghanistan are by now banned from accessing education, working, playing sports, or going to the park. Women in Iran have been protesting for their rights since months, courageously challenging the power and religion structures that hold them back, and are being imprisoned, tortured, poisoned, abused. And many other women across the world are courageously resisting, protesting, organising to dismantle a system that pushes them down.

"I feel for those women. I understand them . . . I am one of them", says Tawakkol—conscious of the obstacles and the harassments she has had to face as a female activist back in her home country, where she no longer lives exactly for these reasons. "I can share what I had to face . . . maybe it's helpful for other women, for those who are today fighting these battles?" she asks. Before I have the time to say "of course", Tawakkol starts speaking again, sharing a structured analysis of the challenges she has dealt with.

"I had to face three issues: the religion, the dictator, and the culture. They are connected, true, but they are three issues and it's helpful to understand how you can tackle each of them".

BREAKING DOWN BARRIERS: RELIGION

"Let me start with the religion. Or, let me say it better . . . let me start with the religious views on the participation of women in public life: this was the hardest thing among the three. But as a premise, let me say for who doesn't know my story that I am religious, I believe in Islam—very deeply. And it doesn't stop there: I am someone who appreciates all religions, I respect them, I study them. As someone who knows them and believes in them, I can say with confidence that the problems we have in our societies are not with religions *per se*, but with the people who explain and translate them in an extreme way. And this happens in all religions. Christianity suffered from that in the Middle Age: they sent crusaders to the Middle East for over two centuries, to take the Holy Land away from Muslim control. The same thing is happening with the Jews, and with how they want to impose their religion and their state over the Palestinians. And we are having the same problem since a few decades within Islam . . . you must have seen during your time in the Middle East the rise of the Islamic State (ISIS), the terrorists' attacks, and much more".

I nod, as personal memories from that time come back to mind. I see colleagues and friends who were murdered or tortured by ISIS while we were working in Iraq and Syria during the war . . . *in the name of what?* That is a question that always comes back to my mind when thinking of my years living in and working on the humanitarian crisis in Syria, Iraq and the neighbouring countries—filled with beautiful and horrible memories at the same time. Luckily, Tawakkol continues to explain her perspective, distracting me from these thoughts: "Again, it's important to understand that the problem is not the religion, but the people who put themselves in the middle of the person and their God, who believe they are the interpreters of God. They are not, what they are is a tool of tyrannies, which are using Islam to force women to play a traditional role and men to abide by certain rules. Those people are not independent, they are part of an orchestrated effort—and I gathered a lot of evidence of it during my experiences as a journalist, a politician, and an activist in Yemen. Those people take orders from national security, from intelligence and dictators—orders which often go against what their religion or their God actually says. It's as simple as this: Islam is not what they claim it is", says Tawakkol in a solemn voice. "My religion is a religion of peace, of justice, of equality. A religion which in no way discriminates against woman, and which is fully compatible with human rights and democracy. A religion from which we could all learn so much—if only it wouldn't be suffocated by extremists. An extreme fringe that silences the moderate majority, that terrorises us, that occupies the headlines on media and key positions in government, that turns religion into a control tool for regimes. And of course, this part of the Muslim story is the only one you see in Western media—which creates even more fears, ever deeper divisions and misunderstandings between Christian countries and Muslim ones".

"Well, now that I have done this 'short' premise", says Tawakkol in an ironic tone, "I can tell you that facing these religious people was the most difficult thing of all. I had to tell them they do not represent our religion, that their views are not right. I had to reject their framework of Islam. And, in parallel, I had to convince women of it as well, to get them on my side, to encourage them to lead a revolution against those men, and against Islam as a tool for tyranny. It was hard, very hard to face this religious component, but I had to. I spoke out against early marriage, in favour of mixed women and men participation in the public sphere—starting from our demonstrations. And while I was doing that, the Imams—who led the prayers across the mosques in Yemen—and the Sheiks would call me out, saying that what I was doing was *haram*, I don't know how to say that in English"—"a *sin*, or *something forbidden*—not sure either how to best translate it", I say, and she laughs saying she now has the proof I lived in the Middle East. "In any case", she continues, "standing up against this religion part—as a Muslim woman, which sees Islam as a source of guidance for her activism, and which believes that it can be a force for positive change in the world—was the most important and the most risky challenge. Without that though I wouldn't have managed to change the other two parts: the dictatorship and the culture".

BREAKING DOWN BARRIERS: THE DICTATOR

"Let's move to the battle against the dictator, my second challenge". Tawakkol takes a deep breath, as I try to imagine what it would mean to stand up against a dictator, also if only for a second. I wonder where we, as a single human being, find this incredible courage and conviction to fight against what seems unmovable, powerful, dangerous. And I tell myself that this conversation sounds a little surreal: while I am surrounded by my calm, safe and peaceful European life, I am reminded that people—a few hours away by plane—are fighting against dictators and risking their lives for it.

"The dictator was the person behind this extreme interpretation of Islam, on top of being behind the socioeconomic catastrophe my country was going through. As I was fighting against this wrong interpretation of Islam, I saw how the voices of those extreme people were supported from behind. There are endless numbers of moderate Muslims in Yemen and in the Middle East, but their voices never manage to emerge, to get to the public. Why? Because the media supports extreme voices. And who decides what the media supports? The dictator, the tyrannic system, that was restricting more and more press freedom exactly for this reason. Saleh loved these voices, they were useful for his power, so he made sure only those voices would be heard, highlighted—while silencing all the other voices, like mine. And this reasoning didn't apply only to the freedom of expression, it was across the board. The dictator didn't allow anyone to lead, to speak up—except from his family, his tribe, over which he had complete control", explains Tawakkol. "So how could we overturn these extreme voices? By overturning the dictatorial system behind it—it was as simple as that. We had to overturn the system that was putting me as a woman, as a human being, in a marginalised role. The system which didn't want me to participate in public life as a citizen. And I could get there only by doing what, according to the system, was considered *haram*—by speaking out, by protesting, by being a visible woman in public life. And thanks to the mobilisation of the people, men and women, we succeeded in doing just that. Of course", she adds with a saddened look, "only until when the counter-revolution started . . . but even on this, we must think positive: the counter-revolution is a natural consequence to a revolution, history teaches us just that. This means it's a matter of time before the counter-revolution will be over and we'll hopefully be able to install a democratic and peaceful system in Yemen. A system in which religion and state are completely separate entities—I want to be very clear on this", explains Tawakkol. "We need a state in which religion does not interfere with the governmental system, while ensuring the state respects all religions as well as those who don't believe in religion. We need clear laws and guarantees to ensure the separation of these two entities. This is the only way in which religion and democracies can and should coexist, and I hope this day will come sooner rather than later for my country also".

BREAKING DOWN BARRIERS: THE CULTURE

"But the challenges don't end here". Her voice sounds very patient—as if this accumulation of problems is simply part of reality and there is no way around it. "Even when we overturned the dictator, and managed to provide a different framework for Islam, we still needed to deal with a deeply ingrained culture, with traditions and costumes that hold women back. According to the dominant culture, a woman in Yemen is meant to play only the traditional role: serving the house, serving her father, serving her brother—not even serving her mother or her sisters . . . it's all about serving the men. Tradition doesn't want women to shine, to have a voice, to be emancipated, independent. And dismantling those traditions takes a long time. But I had someone who helped me to deal with this, guess who?" "The Queen?", I say. "Yes, she is my constant reminder this is not in our blood, meaning it is possible to dismantle this last part of our broken system, and we are working on it!", she adds with a confident smile.

"These three obstacles defined me, shaped what my role was going to be: to destroy these actors, to lead my people to confront them, freeing my country from the dictator, from religious extremism and from outdated traditions". Tawakkol takes a moment to think, to formulate her thoughts. "My advice to others who are fighting such battles, and to all those who will fight them in the future, as small or as big as they can be, is when you face an obstacle, don't stop your journey, don't get frustrated, discouraged. Rather use that obstacle to define yourself against it, to strengthen your role, to use it as a source of power, not as something that takes power away from you. And don't give up until you find a way of overcoming that obstacle, until you find freedom. Because that's what leadership is and that's what our world needs".

And that obstacle, in Tawakkol's case, is still there. Freedom is not a reality for her people and her country—meaning her fight is not over. So we switch from her past, her story, to the future, her future.

Tawakkol was, as of 2011, the youngest woman ever—aged 32—to receive the Nobel Peace Prize, becoming the first Arab woman and the first Yemeni to receive this award. Meaning she still has many, many, years ahead of her to continue bringing change. "I'll stick to my role", she says as if that's a given. "I'll face dictators in the Arab region, until we become real democracies. I'll continue helping revolutions around the world, until the last dictator is gone. It's a big job but we'll get there. And it's not the only job to be done . . . I hope I will also succeed in helping democratic countries to protect their own democracies. This means protecting freedom of speech, re-establishing facts, and working against polarisation. This is why I joined the Meta [former Facebook] Supervisory Board: to secure freedom of speech and protect our collective lives, online and offline. Protecting today's democracies though also means helping them to stop working with dictators around the world: they weaken themselves and they strengthen the dictators each time they do so. Staying true to democratic values is a *sine qua non* for the future of democracy and for the future of the world".

Not surprisingly, Tawakkol has clear-cut ideas on the role she wants to play in our world and on how to fix the interconnected challenges we are facing: democracy, autocracy, polarisation, rights, extremism, war, and peace.

"Ah, and I also do something else", she adds as an afterthought, but as soon as she starts speaking about it, her eyes light up. "I am working in the field of development. I created the Tawakkol Karman Foundation which focuses mainly on Yemen. We work on education—the key to the future. Building schools, providing scholarships for youth, teaching them English so they can learn from the world. Imagine", she says with shiny eyes, "we have 7000 students studying English right now. And we also work on health, on access to water . . . you know, the basic services for kids to grow healthy and be able to focus on school. It's important to work in development, just as you do with your organisation. But, I do have a but", she adds with a smile, "if we succeed in ensuring all countries are ruled by a good governance, then governments would take care of schools, of hospitals, of halting injustice and inequality, between women and men as well. If we could replace all dictators with democratic leaders, capable and driven by values, development aid will no longer be needed. *Inshallah*, this will be reality one day—but we need many other revolutions to happen to reach our collective freedom".

The doorbell rings as Tawakkol is still finishing her sentence. It rings again, and this time she looks down at her watch. "Oh! I am late for my next appointment", she says. I turn off the recording and we quickly say goodbye. I leave feeling as if our encounter, our conversation is suspended in a limbo: I still have tons of questions floating in my mind, a long list of things she said I would want to unpack, to understand her better, to go deeper beyond the iron curtain, to feel sure I am channelling as I should her character and her vision to the world. But time—in this case—is not on our side.

As I write this chapter, listening on repeat to the recording of our conversation, reading interviews, speeches, articles, and anything I can find online about Tawakkol's life, I slowly manage to close the loop, to fill the gaps, to put an end to what felt like a suspended conversation. And while doing so, I feel always more clearly her strength coming through. Her determination, her laser-focus approach, her clear-mindedness in everything she does or speaks of: be it the history of her Queen, her belief in Islam as a religion of peace, her life trajectory, her vision for our world today, and for how women and youth are the beacons of hope to fix it.

I tell myself that these must be the traits of a true revolutionary: the braveness and the integrity to stick to one's path and one's cause, no matter the obstacles, setbacks or threats we might receive. Leadership is also this: this revolutionary skill of sticking to our dreams, of combining what exists with what has not existed before—be it within a family, a community, or a country. And I tell myself that by dreaming of a different world, of Tawakkol's "free world", we'll manage to transform it into reality—one revolution at a time.

· 6 ·

INTEGRITY
Comfort Ero

IT WAS A GREY week in November 2022. I had recently started my new job—as the managing director of an international foundation—and was in Paris for the first days with the team. After four days of back-to-back meetings, I decide at the last minute to stay one more day and attend a large peace forum that is hosted each year in the stock exchange palace in the heart of Paris, hoping to get some insights into how to position the ambition of my new organisation into the peace and security debates at the European level.

A former colleague and friend is in charge of running part of the forum's programme, and during one of the coffee breaks, he offers me the chance to join his next meeting: a closed-door discussion with the newly appointed CEO of the International Crisis Group (ICG). "*Elle est trop forte*", he says in French ["she is very cool" for the non-French-speaking]. Positively surprised by the fact that it's a "she", in a sector in which women occupying leadership positions is rare, I say yes. And on the way to the meeting room, I start asking questions. "Her name is Comfort Ero", he says, as I try to remember if we ever crossed paths in my previous roles, or if I saw her on TV or in some newspaper. "She is British–Nigerian", he adds, "and no, she wasn't a well-known personality before".

Typically, CEOs of the Crisis Group, and of equivalent organisations within the international relations and international development fields come from eminent political positions. Former prime ministers, ministers, or senior advisors to heads of states are the usual candidates to take on the top leadership role. And despite the change of sector, they continue acting as such: surrounded by staff carrying briefs and bags, nodding at people while walking—aware of their notoriety, while keeping that VIP-type of distance which they learned to build along the way. And when in meetings, they usually give an address, lecturing others about their vision of the world, all while carefully weighing every single word they say in case the media picks on it, to then run off to the next event. This is why I expected to recognise her name. "She is different from the others. In a good way . . . wait and see", says my friend with a smile—trying to appease my curiosity.

We come across Comfort in the corridor as she is trying to find her way in this huge building: my friend quickly introduces us as we continue walking towards the meeting room. She is alone, and during the meeting, she is completely herself. Comfort acts nothing like the usual suspect for someone in this position. She first wants to know everyone's names, what we do. To then share a few ideas to kick off a dialogue, not a lecture. And as she speaks, with a calm and discrete tone, I discover she doesn't come, as her predecessors, from high-level government positions, but from within the organisation.

Comfort is an analyst—as are the majority of her colleagues in the ICG—and she has, over 20 years, slowly but surely moved up the ranks, and is now the first-ever CEO with this insider profile. An insider which, since the end of 2021—just a few months before the beginning of the war in Ukraine—was given the reins of one of the most notorious non-profits working on conflict prevention and peacebuilding: their reports are on the desks of heads of state, informing decisions of governments, of international bodies, with the hope to de-escalate wars, build peace, and prevent new conflicts from erupting across the globe. It's a job in which you need to have the credibility and courage to speak truth to power and to dialogue with whoever is in front of you: war lords, authoritarian heads of states, rebel leaders. A job in which you must build common ground with everyone, if you hope to end or prevent conflict.

"I never doubt the mandate, the mission of the Crisis Group", Comfort explains with a shy but convinced look on her face. "And to honour this mission, also means speaking to people who have blood on their hands. To gain their trust, their confidence, as they are the parties to any conflict and, without them onboard, we cannot end wars—wherever they may be. We must keep going, and I feel honoured to have been given the responsibility of doing just that: safeguarding and advancing Crisis Group's important mission in a moment where our world needs peace more than ever".

The hour we have together in Paris flies by. As we walk towards the exit, I quickly pitch to her this book and explain I would love to have her voice in it. We exchange contact information, and five months later, we manage to come together again— always on a grey day, this time in London.

We meet up at the entrance of the ICG office. I expect this to be a buzzing space, filled with analysts, rushing to finalise reports about conflicts, peace deals, negotiations, geopolitical shifts. Instead, it's a few offices in a large co-working space. It's a Friday morning, and Comfort seems to be the only one there. Her office is small, white, anonymous. It holds her desk, her desktop, a second desk and desk chair, no plants, no pictures, no personal belongings. "I come here when I am in London", she explains as I look around. "We are maybe 10 to 12 colleagues in the UK but mostly we are home based. The headquarters are in Brussels, but you know", she explains in her stark British accent, "I was born in London, my family is here, so was happy at the idea of staying based in the UK. The rest of my time I spend travelling, to visit our teams, understand what happens on the ground, and relay it to decision-makers across the world in various international summits and meetings".

We both sit with our cups of English breakfast tea, across the two desks in this unpretentious office. Comfort moves the monitor to her left so we can see each other better—I take out my notebook, recorder and questionnaire, and we start talking.

IT STARTS AT HOME

"Where my leadership comes from?", says Comfort repeating my first question. "I grew up in a household led by formidable women: my mother and my aunties. The way these women raised us, their children, is what built the basis of who I am. They taught us to be upstanding, to be proud, but also to be fair, to be just, to be equitable. That's where I learned how to build myself, how to be humble and respectful of other people. And that's where my understanding of leadership came from. My family taught me how to treat other human beings, share responsibilities, organise my life, and support others, my church, my community, while always remembering where we came from, our roots, and our upbringing".

"You see", explains Comfort with a shy look on her face—as if she is not used to sharing her personal life story, "my parents came from Nigeria. They moved to the UK in the 1960s, along with many other young people who were hoping to get an education abroad. They actually met in London, discovered themselves here, not in Nigeria, while my father was studying science and my mother was training to become a nurse. Once they finished their studies, they both really wanted to go back to Nigeria, build their life together there. But the civil war erupted, and their parents advised them to stay abroad. In Nigeria, there was a general lack of opportunities, not the easiest place to raise a family, and my mum's parents told her that having part of the family outside of Nigeria was going to become an important pipeline for other relatives, nieces, and nephews, to grow, get an education, and leave Nigeria if things ever got worse. They were that pipeline, that pathway, so my parents stayed put in London, where my brothers and I were born. They were stubborn people though", she adds with an affectionate smile, "and still wanted their children—two at the time—to be brought up in Nigeria, in the Nigerian way of life. I was only an infant when my parents sent us back to Nigeria to live with my aunties, while they remained in London as the family pipeline".

I look a little surprised, since I come from a typical Western culture where, as much as we like repeating the African proverb "it takes a village to raise a child", our reality is often far from it. It's two parents, balancing work and childcare, often struggling to hold everything together.

Comfort smiles and explains that for years, she was convinced that her biological parents were the ones in Nigeria, not the ones in London, to make me understand the extent to which "the village approach" was normal in her case. "In Nigerian culture, we sometimes refer to relations based on where they are located. In Nigeria, I was looked after by aunty—my mum's eldest sister, who was living on the campus of Lagos University, where her husband worked as registrar. She was a sociologist, a museum curator, in charge of the African American Institute. I called them "mummy and daddy *campus*". We had our own teacher for schooling but were sometimes shuttled from Lagos to Ibadan, a city four hours away, where I would stay with my mum's brother and his wife. She ran a school, where I could be with other children. It was a great life—it was everything I knew. But Nigeria was going through difficult times, and it was decided my brother and I should go back to London.

In my mind, it meant leaving my real parents, mummy and daddy *campus*. Once back in London—to do my last year at pre-school—it took me a while to realise that "mummy and daddy *London*" were not some faraway relatives but my biological parents", she says with a loud laugh. "I feel I have had, throughout my life, several sets of parents. In our culture, this is a matter of respect—but it is also something that truly enriched me. It gave me multiple reference points, allowed me to be raised by a village, between London, Lagos, and Ibadan. I then stayed in London throughout school and university, but always kept a strong bond and curiosity towards Nigeria", says Comfort, fast-forwarding in time, "a curiosity which shaped my studies and career path".

REUNITING WHAT IS DIVIDED

Comfort has always been fascinated by history, with a particular curiosity for the Berlin Wall and for Nigeria's internal divisions. She is intrigued by relations between states and between people. "I mean, think of my grandparents: they told their daughter not to come home, to stay outside, because of the conflict in Nigeria. Don't you find that intriguing? What drives society to fight against itself?", she says with a spark in her voice—unveiling her curious analyst soul. "I was doing my degree in London at the time of the end of the Cold War. A continent, partly my continent—Europe, had been divided for decades. The Berlin Wall seemed unmovable, unbreakable: it was all I knew since I was born, a divisive line between two worlds. And then, overnight, it falls. How can that happen? What does that falling wall mean for Germans, for Jews, for Europeans, for the rest of the world? How did it make them feel? Happy to be reunited? I was so fascinated by its collapse. I spent so many nights while in university reading the news and studying it. I was so fascinated because it made me think of my country of origin, Nigeria". Comfort's voice gets heavier, her black eyes look deeper. "I remember the feeling when I left Lagos as a six-year-old. The feeling of fleeing, rushing to the airport, being obliged to leave everything I ever knew behind to move to a country I didn't know—the UK. All because there were rumours of a potential coup. That feeling stuck with me, and it re-emerged throughout my life each time I saw on television people fleeing, suffering, be it in Latin America, in Africa, or anywhere else in the world. So, to me, the fall of the Berlin Wall, gave me hope that I didn't have: change can happen, divided countries can unite, broken societies can be rebuilt. And it gave me the hope that all of this could happen also back in Nigeria, despite the civil war, the divisions between groups of society".

Comfort stops speaking for a moment to ask if I have ever been to Nigeria. I have travelled a lot for work, including in Sub-Saharan Africa, but never to Nigeria. I know the map of Nigeria, as we had a team based all the way in the north-east—close to the border with Niger and Chad, in the city of Maiduguri—and I would often be in touch with them from my Geneva office for programmatic and security checks given the instability of the area. I know of Nigerian pop music, as my Nigerian classmate at university had it on constant repeat on her TV in the student dorms we lived in; and I know about their super-spicy and slimy food—I remember turning completely red after the first spoon of a soup, in the same student dorm. That is my level of knowledge. "Well", says Comfort, amused by my stereotypical data points on Nigeria, "it has all of the above! But it's a country that went through a lot of conflict and suffering".

Inhabited since thousands of years, Nigeria saw the rise and fall of numerous empires, until it came under British control in the 1860s, becoming a formal British colony in 1914. "It took us nearly 60 years to regain our independence: we became a Republic in 1963", explains Comfort. "But the impact of colonialisation, layered with power, competition and ethnic divisions over the vision for Nigeria led to military coups and civil war". There are three main groups in Nigeria: the Hausa-Fulani in the north, the Igbos in the east, the Yorubas in the west. Regional leaders protected their tribes, their privileges, creating endemic competition between these areas—a competition which sometimes escalated into conflict. This means that building a unified country wasn't an easy task: disagreements led, in 1967, to the eastern regions declaring their independence—forming the Republic of Biafra. The central government saw it as an act of rebellion, and this disagreement transformed into a full-fledged civil war. "The civil war shaped my personal history, the decisions of my family, where I was brought up". Comfort explains the history of her country as her own personal story, helping me see that when someone has a passion for it, history is not only something for the books, but a tool to understand our life and our world.

"You heard of Biafra, right?", she asks. I nod, as everyone working in humanitarian aid—as I did—had heard of it, time, and time again: it symbolises a turning point in the history of humanitarian aid. Images of starving children from Biafra created a wave of solidarity and rushed donations from the global north. Church organisations from all over the world came together to create an aid alliance and supply food and medicine to a population which was being starved to death. They organised the largest civilian airlift in history: 7,000 flights with lifesaving supplies. An airlift larger than the more famous Berlin airlift after the Second World War. But the aid provided was far from sufficient. The civil war in Nigeria ended in 1970 with the surrender of the Republic of Biafra, exhausted by the starvation and the ethnic cleansing of its people, the Igbos, with deaths estimated to be in the millions.

"The harm and the horror inflicted on people in the Biafra region, the outrageous humanitarian tragedy, these are things that stuck with me, that run in my DNA as I listened to relatives describe the war. I always wondered how human beings can inflict all this pain on another human. And for what?", says Comfort with a severe look. "I'll say more. The problem lies not only in what happens during a conflict, such as the one in Biafra, but also in what happens—or doesn't happen rather—after the end of it. After every war, people, communities, countries, must deal with the grievances, otherwise they just continue to resurge. Truth is we didn't properly deal with that aspect, with reconciliation, justice, grievances, in the case of Biafra, and that partly explains why even today we see ethnic and religious tensions emerging time and time again in Nigeria. You understand now?", she asks while connecting the dots of her reasoning, "this is why I was fascinated by the fall of the Berlin Wall: I saw it as a chance to learn how people go about rebuilding a society, reconstructing relations, halting polarisation, consolidating peace. And how that could be done back in Nigeria, or in any of the crises we saw on our TV screens during those years". The excitement in Comfort's eyes, her vision on how we could build instead of blow up bridges, lasts just a few seconds.

"Let's not forget", adds Comfort as an important afternote, "that my university years were also the years of the genocide in Rwanda. I remember feeling frozen in time, speechless, when that happened. After Biafra, the international community said 'never again'. After apartheid, we said 'never again'. I had been told by my parents, my professors, that my generation was going to be at an advantage: end of the Cold War, end of the nuclear race, end of the apartheid. And here we were, just a few years later, with a massacre happening in front of our eyes, broadcasted on radio and TV screens, and with the international system failing yet again to intervene, to stop the genocide, to save millions of lives. This moment of relief, this moment of change, this hope that we were witnessing in Europe with the fall of the Berlin Wall was brought down in a matter of seconds by what happened in Rwanda. As a young adult, this deeply shaped my outlook on the world".

I am sure many people from Comfort's generation were impacted by these events, and many others lived through history without even noticing it was happening—occupied by their daily worries and desires. This is the case for every generation. And a bunch of us, from each generation, cannot not only look away while history, injustices are happening but also cannot think of doing anything else until the problems we see in our world are fixed. Comfort is one of these people. She shares that these events are the reason why she started asking herself questions: where are the institutions, the mechanisms, the leaders that are meant to stop this from happening? Why are we failing, so blatantly, to make "never again" a reality all over the world? "I couldn't not question the inadequacy of our institutions, starting from the United Nations. And this inadequacy is exactly what drove me towards what I am doing every day with my work: transforming these institutions, informing leaders' decisions, making this 'never again' a reality for all".

Having worked in contexts of crises myself, in countries where this "never again" is far from being applied, be it Syria, Ethiopia, or Myanmar, and having dealt with the many frustrating shortcomings of the international governance system—starting from the United Nations—I can't resist asking Comfort where she finds hope.

"You, I, people like us, we just can't lose hope. If we lose the belief that things can be changed, that the system can be improved, that wars can be avoided, that conflict can be ended . . . well, if we lose that hope, we give up. And we give up on millions of people who need us to show up for them", says Comfort in a voice filled with courage. "In short, the minute we stop hoping, we fail—so we simply don't have the luxury to do that", she adds with a reassuring smile. "But I don't want to sound too negative. I do see real opportunities, possibilities, in my job—every single day. Open windows for peace-making, for justice. Incremental attempts for de-escalation of conflict even in the toughest countries we work in. This is what helps me go forward, keeping the hope alive. And of course, despite all its shortcomings, I still have hope for the United Nations, and a strong belief in the UN Charter: it binds us all, as humanity. This body was born out of war, to prevent it from happening again, and we must ensure it does just that. That deep belief in the UN mandate is actually what drove the very first steps of my career", explains Comfort. "A UN internship brought me to West Africa. The region was going through turbulences, be it in Liberia, Sierra Leone, or Ivory Coast. And I wanted to help contribute to stopping these wars. And I haven't stopped ever since!"

"You know?", says Comfort while looking straight into my eyes. "I always felt in me this desire to contribute to society, to peace. I felt it as I started my first internship, and it is the case till today as the head of the ICG. And this desire to lead change, this purpose, is driven by my education, my family background, which defined what leadership looks like to me".

Comfort's mother was a believer in people's goodness: if you treat people well, they will do the same to you. "This belief is entrenched in me—it taught me and shaped me more than any theory. And this belief in goodness is what gives me the hope, the stamina for doing the type of work I do. My mother wanted me to turn up and be good to people. To be honourable because she came from an honourable family. That's how she raised her children. This is where my understanding of leadership and character came from. And this is why I expect a leader, yes, to be a visionary, but even more to show up in a good, honourable, honest way: to show people through your character that you seek to be inclusive, to listen, to be transparent, to be held accountable, to be good. This is what makes you a leader". Integrity sums up Comfort's vision of leadership. "Yes", she says, "integrity is what gives you the power to bring change, to inspire others, to create new pathways for collaboration, for peace. And that's the type of leader I try to be every day. . ." says Comfort. "I don't know if I succeed, but at least I try", she adds while laughing out loud.

DIFFERENT

Comfort to me feels different from most of the leaders I have met in my life. Of course, she is a black woman in a sector and a world dominated by white men. But the difference goes way beyond this evident diversity she brings to the table. "I am very aware that previous CEOs didn't look like me", she admits. "There are a few of us at the top, in academic institutions and government. I recently met with the vice president of Colombia—the first Afro-Colombian—so change is happening, but we are still too few". That is undeniably the case. Though she also feels different to me in another way: more reflective, more discrete, more attentive, less outgoing, less loud, less assertive. At least compared to the average CEOs or senior political figures I have encountered through my work.

"Maybe it's because I am the middle child?", she says with a kind smile on her face. "The older brother with whom I went to Nigeria as a kid is one year older, the other is six years younger. Believe me, being the middle child shapes you. You see the future through your older sibling, the battles, the tactics, what worked, what hasn't. You learn the risks, the consequences of certain actions, and you use that to inform your strategy. But at the same time, you play a role towards the younger one: you mediate, you inform them of what is coming next, you mentor them. I was stuck in the middle: trying to iron things out between the future and the past. And this is perhaps where I got this attentive, discrete, aware part of my character from. It has served me well so far", adds Comfort while somehow seeking a sign of reassurance.

"In any case", she continues, "I would want to see more of this in leadership. More capacity to listen rather than to talk, to bridge divides rather than to create them, to help teams achieve their goals rather than impose our goals on them. And I think this is what helped me move up the ranks within Crisis Group. When I took over the Africa programme, I didn't come in to impose a certain idea on others, rather I came in to help the analysts achieve what they wanted to achieve within the organisation's mandate. And even now, as president and CEO, I am a facilitator, with a vision to evolve our organisation in the midst of a tense geopolitical climate. Someone who has been given the honour to safeguard the organisational mandate, to protect it, make it grow, also by giving my team the space to thrive, to fulfil the ambition they have for themselves—as long as it's rooted in our overall mandate. And to do so, until the day that I'll hand the ICG over to my successor, hopefully stronger and more impactful than before. I hope at least that's what my colleagues would say if you asked them about my leadership, about how I got to where I am—despite not having walked my predecessors' corridors of power and despite not looking like those that came before me".

Comfort confesses she was herself genuinely surprised when she got the job—exactly because she is different. She was confirmed as the new CEO at the end of 2021, during the COVID-19 pandemic, in the aftermath of the #blacklivesmatter and #metoo movements. There were already significant conversations going on in the world about what leadership looks like and Comfort explains there was a desire for a different kind of leadership.

It is interesting that this push to revise what leadership means and looks like didn't come from the top: the top, of course, doesn't want to give up its power, so it will never come from there. It came from the people. We tend to spend a lot of time looking at leadership in terms of state leadership, which is failing us in many ways: democracies and rights are shrinking, autocracies and violence are increasing, populism and anti-migrants' walls are becoming common currency. But while this layer of leadership is failing, creating polarisation, turbulence, something has been moving at another level: the grassroots one.

"I remember so vividly the moment I saw the video of George Floyd". Comfort pauses, as if she is trying to jump back into that instant. "We were all in lockdown. At home. Some of us working, some looking after our children, some left without a job. But every one of us was standing still. And we all saw the horror of that video, which could circulate broadly because of the digital age we are living in. A horror that spread nationwide in the US to then become international, because the problem of abuse of power against marginalised groups is everywhere, whatever that group might be. People turned out on the streets in some countries, including where I live—the UK—and familiar conversations on police brutality, on violence, on race were unfolding. And in those conversations, we started speaking of diversity, of inclusion, of empathy. These issues aren't new, but the pandemic added another layer of complexity, and politics was increasingly polarising communities in countries such as the UK and US". The language of diversity, of empathy, of inclusion, came from the bottom, from people like you, like me, our families, and friends. It didn't come from the big palaces of power. And it's a language that carries power. It forced the so-called "leaders" of nations, of companies, to think differently, to become inclusive, to deal with institutional racism and discrimination—be it towards minorities or women.

"Of course, George Floyd was not the only tragedy" continues Comfort. "There have been many others before and unfortunately there will be more in the future. But all these issues were bound up in this tragic 10-second video". A video which young people and others used as a tool to seek a transformation, to push for different leadership across the world. And there have been several of these types of moments over the past years. There is an impetus for change, driven from the bottom, from a human consciousness of our rights and responsibilities, across nations, which is pushing changes in leadership at the top level. "I am of course so happy to see it happening, but with deep divide and marginalisation in so many societies, even in rich advanced countries, I am sceptical about change", concludes Comfort.

She's acutely aware that her appointment comes at a time when employees expect leaders to better handle staff well-being and diversity. "Institutions are speaking of staff well-being, because of the impact of COVID-19; of racism because it was further highlighted by the George Floyd murder; and of diversity because of the #MeToo movement. We have our work cut out, much remains at stake because there's much to change, but we cannot ignore these demands for change. And I am honoured to be in the position where I can hopefully bring about positive change", she adds with a proud look.

Comfort is also cognisant of being the first woman of colour at the helm of the organisation, though not the first woman. "It feels scary", admits Comfort, her voice a bit shaky. "You learn very quickly as a woman of colour how to protect yourself. You are constantly being validated: people wonder 'will she be capable of it?'. And you are always questioned: 'is she in this position only because of her gender, of her skin colour?'". As she speaks these words, I feel the weight on her shoulders. But her serious eyes become a little lighter, as she switches to another train of thought. "Luckily, I have been blessed with many people who believed in me, who promoted me because they saw I was capable of leading". But let's be honest . . . despite all the advances, people like Comfort remain rare. As she nods, Comfort adds that this is why she wants to use her personal accomplishment to do good: "to help others stand on my shoulders, just as I stood on the shoulders of those who supported me every step of the way".

Comfort's layers of diversity don't end here though. As she explained, she came from within the organisation, which made the transition to the top more complex. "From one day to the next, your peers are no longer your peers. You feel under immense pressure. You hold the ultimate responsibility, the weight, the implications of decisions, and that can feel lonely. I admit that sometimes I sit in this office by myself struggling to decide what the best final call is. Or simply struggling to get out of my mind competing demands and interests, trying to make sure that I can hear my own voice, that I can lean in the direction that feels right to me, and avoid getting lost in what others want and focus on what's important for the health of the organisation and for myself. But all in all, if I count the number of times I have felt alone since taking on this position, it's very few. Because I also know that I am working with allies, within and outside the organisation. It's an organisation of big brains and big minds that are supportive of our common goal, of our mandate to prevent and end conflicts. And that is what creates the unity we need to lead change within our world".

WHAT IS LEFT TO DO

We continue sharing experiences, anecdotes, tips, on what it means to be at the top. And while doing so, Comfort opens up about her fears. "First, I am seen as a nice person. You spotted it too, quickly, and pointed it out. I am not outwardly pushy, someone who exerts her position". Sometimes, more shy, quieter personalities find themselves being used to service other people's agenda, and she tells me she has learned the hard way how to safeguard herself. "I am wary of this", says Comfort, "for myself and for other colleagues who have a similar character as mine". She also worries about "projecting" her own insecurity onto others. "We all suffer insecurities, it's natural, but what I have learned with time is to make sure they don't impact our relations with others—and to check ourselves and make sure we are not doing just that". Being aware of our vulnerabilities, our insecurities, and of how they can play in our relationships—be it at work or at home—requires a lot of self-knowledge and self-awareness, but it's a crucial part of how we relate to others. And that is especially true when you are in a leadership position.

Comfort takes another quick break, as she reflects on what she has just said, on her own insecurities and vulnerabilities. She plays a bit with the cord of her monitor, and starts again: "Comfort, don't be so strict with yourself, otherwise you'll miss out on the good moments of life", she tells herself while imitating a deeper and more authoritative voice than hers. "Yes, I am now the head of the organisation; I have achieved something I aspired to for a long time. Sure, the scrutiny is higher, the risks are higher . . . but I must take the time to enjoy what I have accomplished and use this opportunity wisely— this is the advice I would give to myself, to try not to overfocus on my own vulnerabilities and insecurities".

I joke that it would be amazing if only we would be as good at listening to our own advice, as we were at giving it to others. Comfort laughs along and mentions often sharing advice with others that she wishes she would apply to herself. "One tip I give to colleagues who are stepping into leadership roles and that I would want to share with anyone reading these words and hoping to lead their communities or their organisations is to never see the problem at hand as the issue. The issue is how you manage or don't manage the problem, never the problem *per se*. Problems are everywhere, they are not a testament of your character. The real test of your leadership is how you deal with them, and if you own the decisions you take and their consequences, without blaming others. That's how I see my role, and how I would want to be judged from those coming after me".

Comfort regularly comes back to her role, to how she is perceived by her colleagues, and to how her legacy will be perceived in the future. I can see that compared to other leaders I have spoken to for this book—some of whom held high-level roles and are now in the giving back phase—things for her are different. She is in the midst of her career, occupied by her current tasks and decisions as CEO, wondering about what will come next and what she will leave behind.

She also regularly comes back to the ICG's mission, centred around the concept of prevention rather than cure. A philosophy of life which, in my view, is sorely lacking in today's definition of "leadership". "War is not inevitable. It's a man-made disaster, and it can be fixed by men and women, by us. This is our starting point", explains Comfort. "This notion that we have no choice but to go to war, which is what you see at play now between Ukraine and Russia, is untrue". And indeed, on the eve of the first attack on Ukraine, experts—including those from the ICG—were laying down options and scenarios that were necessary and plausible to halt the start of the war.

As she speaks of these topics, Comfort's voice gains depth and authoritativeness—she enters her comfort zone. "What we try to do is to develop policy that speaks both to the reality on the ground and to the trade-offs international actors must make, while looking for the ideal. Because on this we must be pragmatic: there is the ideal, and there is the reality. And trade-offs, compromises, are part of policy and decision-making, are part of daily life: they are the only way to blend the ideal and the reality together. We don't see the inevitability of anything, so our job is to constantly search for solutions—and this is part of what leadership should be: searching for the common ground. This means that our analysis gets us in front of decision-makers, and that is when we start building the case for different pathways to peace, or to de-escalation, or to avoiding conflict altogether. But if we want to avoid getting into these dramatic crisis situations in the first place, what we really need is a shift of mindset in leaders".

If you ask today's leaders, from north to south, from the public and the private sector, most will tell you they see more risk involved in acting early as opposed to acting in the moment of crisis, or often they simply have no incentives in acting early as their mandate in office, in a company, is too short to be concerned by the consequences of a problem which is, as of now, only on the horizon. But this comes with very high costs, in terms of the lives we lose, of heritage destroyed, of consequences for our planet. "The least costly approach is to act early, there is no doubt about this", confirms Comfort. "We must start crafting leaders' mindset to think about what can be done today in order to avoid negative consequences tomorrow. And we must create incentives and mechanisms to hold today's leader to account for how their decisions will impact our collective future". And indeed, this constant "here and now" mentality to decision-making is partly what brought us to the tragic situation our world is in, surrounded by conflicts, climate change, poverty, inequalities; and it's what needs to change if we want to get out of it.

While speaking to these issues, Comfort has a security, a clarity, a direction, which I hadn't perceived before. And which makes me want to hear more.

GLOBAL LEADERSHIP, FOR A RENEWED GLOBAL ORDER

I pick up on her mention of the Russia-Ukraine war, to better grasp her take on today's global world order, as someone who is European and African—split between continents which sometimes feels like two different worlds. "Yeah. . .", she says, "Transforming today's global order is a priority for us all, as the world is changing, and we must evolve with it. This conflict in Ukraine, from my perspective, might already be doing that, but I am not sure yet in which direction".

Indeed, the common perception in the West is that of democracies coming together to defend Ukraine, to stand against authoritarianism, against human rights abuses, for freedom and liberty. Russia, or at least its leaders, embody everything we reject as Western democracies. And countries aligning with Russia, or not condemning its actions openly, are viewed as not standing for our shared values of peace, freedom, democracy. An analysis which, I tell myself, Tawakkol Karman would probably share, given her stark condemnation of countries and, especially, of democracies collaborating with or supporting dictatorships. Comfort, though, shares a more nuanced analysis.

"The Ukraine–Russia war has exposed the fact that the Western global order itself has a lot of internal discrepancies and problems. For decades now, we have been living in a rule-based order. But I've been struck by how many countries are questioning the rule-based order, asking *whose* rules are behind this international order? Those defined by the most powerful countries in the world at the time of the end of the Second World War, which assigned themselves a permanent seat on the Security Council of the United Nations, and the power to veto any decision? The US, the UK, France, but Russia and China too are part of that post–Second World War international order! On top of this, there is some frustration by certain non-Western countries about the fact that Western countries pursue a narrative towards the rest of the world which can be synthesised in: 'do what I say, not what I do'". There's a strong perception that there is one set of rules for Western countries, as protectors of democracy and human rights—despite the abuses, think of George Floyd, the invasion of other countries, think of the US in Iraq, or their internal democracy crises, and one set of rules for the rest of the world: if they do anything along these lines—such as what Russia is doing now in Ukraine—they are condemned. Many of these countries think this double standard is not acceptable: violence should always be condemned, the non-respect of state sovereignty should always be condemned, human rights abuses should always be condemned, not only when Russia does it, these countries argue. "For me, it is unfortunate that these frustrations and reassessment of international relations is happening in the context of the tragedy and aggression against Ukraine, but it is happening, and hopefully it will help build better international cooperation".

We talk about the fact that countries from Africa to Latin America were colonised themselves and know very well what an aggression such as Russia's looks like. They are fully aware of what human suffering is, of how it feels. But they still want to have choices and partnerships with the West, with Russia and with China—and the fact that having such a choice is a priority for them has been a wakeup call for how the West perceives its role in the world. "There's a sense in which European countries and the US are learning for the first time that you must engage these countries on their own terms, not just on Western terms. The West talks of partnership. But the West must enter conversations with others to understand their perspective, what they really mean, and then respect the autonomy of decisions. This is what partnership also looks like", adds Comfort.

"Think of it", she continues in an inquisitive tone. "Most of these countries, when they were at war, were told by Western powers to negotiate. To come to the table. That a military solution is not a solution to a conflict. But they wonder why this logic is not being extended to resolving Ukraine. This moral discrepancy is what gets non-Western countries frustrated". Comfort becomes quiet for a few seconds. When she starts talking again, her tone has changed, it is less warm, more direct, less understanding, more frustrated. "These are the conversations that I am hearing; officials from these non-Western countries argue that their views shouldn't simply be dismissed by Western countries while claiming that Ukraine is different. They also argue that there is a hierarchy of suffering or value on lives lost". Ethiopia was among the deadliest conflict in 2022, for example, and Western countries are prescribing negotiations, peace settlements, ceasefire of hostilities—while asking to supply arms for Ukraine. Hinting, once more, to this discrepancy of priorities and rule-based order.

The capacity of being coherent and adhering to our values, to our principles. The discipline to expect from ourselves what we would like to see from others. The honesty of admitting when we fail to do so. And the courage of engaging with others, to acknowledge and respect their lived experiences and points of view, to then redefine and rediscover a common compass, which should guide and unite us as humanity. In short, it goes back to integrity: this is what I hear behind Comfort's words.

"I wish I would see more of that", confirms Comfort. "More integrity, more respect, more understanding, more willingness to support each other—across countries and cultures—because we are in the same boat. Either we agree on a way of steering it together, or we'll sink it, we will throw it out of balance by fighting on it. Which one do we choose?", she adds with a bitter smile on her face.

WOMEN SUPPORTING WOMEN

"And you know what?", Comfort continues speaking with the same bitterness in her voice. "I wish I would see more of that also among women. Because not all women champion, carry other women. We advocate for equality, for respect, for inclusion, for empowering each other. But often we are exclusive, elitists, not equal. Sometimes some women disempower other women, rather than making sure we lift others up the ladder". As Comfort says these words, I hear her voice getting more fragile. "You touched a raw issue here", she admits with a sweet smile, while taking a moment to pull herself together. She is speaking from experience. "As a black woman in a CEO position, I feel this elitism among those who claim to be inclusive, this hierarchy among those who claim to be empowering. As I said at the very beginning, leadership starts at home. And we must put, within the feminist movements, our home in order—because it is not as inclusive or fair as we claim it to be. And this starts by a few but crucial points. Stop copying masculine models of leadership. Start carrying each other. To show the world what integrity really means, what empowerment really looks like, what respect is. This is the only way we can hope to break the toxic cycle we have all been stuck in, women and men, and to fix the system—for me, for you, and for the generations of women leaders to come".

I ask Comfort about women in leadership and if she had positive and supportive experiences that could serve as examples for people reading these words. "Yes", she responds without hesitation, "that of course has also been the case. One very special group of women dedicated significant time to prepare me for the interview to become president and CEO of Crisis Group. To this group of women, I am indebted for their love and kindness". But she notes, "Several men, including my brother, also helped prepare the ground. Two men, in particular, have been important allies and continue to shape my leadership. Soon after my appointment, a former male colleague, also in leadership, introduced me to a group of women of colour who had been appointed heads of their organisations which was really helpful at the start of my tenure. And overall, be it supporters, friends, Crisis Group's trustees", she adds with a smile, "it was amazing to see how many people were happy for me and what they believe my appointment represents. It's good to be empowered in this way. I've been supported by women coach and stylists too! So I want to give back to others in the way various communities have helped me", she adds.

As Comfort says these words, I am reminded of some research I read about in the *Harvard Business Review*, confirming women and men need different types of networks to succeed. While for men, the key to success lies not in the size of their network but in their centrality within it, i.e. being connected to multiple people with numerous contacts across various groups; for women things look different. We also benefit from being central in our networks, but once we attain executive positions, we require a different type of support: an inner circle of female connections, a close-knit group which can stand with and by us in overcoming the obstacles that men do not typically face. This second type of network is what bolsters a woman's capacity to sustain leadership positions and maximise her impact.

These critical and truthful words of Comfort, on how we too often divide rather than unite among women, become even more pungent knowing research confirms that women do need this type of reciprocal support to succeed and to endure through the many difficulties we face once in executive positions. And need it to make sure we have the capacity to stay within these roles, using them to open doors for other generations of diverse leaders.

At the same time, her words and our shared awareness of the obstacles we face as women leaders, makes the moment we are in feel even more rare, more precious. Two women, two CEOs, engaged in trying to fix our world by navigating the (still manly) corridors of power, taking the time to sit in a small and simple co-working office in the heart of London, with our tea mugs between our hands, sharing experiences, discussing values, imagining how to bridge a divided world and, while doing so, creating a bond capable of amplifying our voices and making us more resilient in our daily tasks.

"Only by supporting each other will we succeed in going far", repeats Comfort as I start packing my stuff, knowing that our two hours of interview are coming to an end and she must run for her next call. We share a complicit smile and start making our way out. Comfort walks me down the corridor and we say goodbye in front of the lift. As I exit the building, I still hear Comfort's voice in my head. Her discrete tone, her laser-sharp focus on her job and organisation, her shyness each time we spoke of more personal things, and her confidence each time we touched a major geopolitical topic.

In all of this, I realise that what sticks with me the most is Comfort's capacity to bring a nuanced view to the table, using this discretion, this observance, this empathy, and this boldness that all coexist in her. Be it about the Russia and Ukraine situation, or about women's empowerment issues: she sees beneath the surface, she goes beyond stereotypes or assumptions, she analyses things inside out to find what needs to change and identify ways of doing just that. And I tell myself that we need more voices like hers around decision-making tables. Because only by bringing them in will we manage to get a new perspective on global problems, and even more a new approach on how to fix them. Only by including these new ways of thinking, acting, and leading will we manage to address the toxic cycle of division, conflict, discrimination, we are all dealing with—be it at home, in the office, or on our TV screens and social media. And only by changing the composition at the decision-making table will we manage to create an environment capable of fostering and welcoming more and more diverse leaders, with large enough shoulders for future generations to stand on.

CIRCULARITY
Gloria Steinem

by Katie Lyman GS

WE ARE BORN INTO a hierarchy. And are taught that to move up, we must identify with that system, the hierarchical mind, rather than change it. The reality though is that things have not always been this way: historically, the power to give birth—on top of all the other capacities women have—used to give women equal power as men, till the moment men started controlling women's wombs, taking power away from them, and increasing their own, starting off what is known as "patriarchy". A system in which dominance and privileges are retained primarily by men and in which those who don't adhere to this hierarchy are stigmatised and marginalised: witches were burned alive because they used herbs to control fertility, and even today, women affirming their rights and their power over their bodies are stigmatised and discriminated against—be it through laws, through family or societal pressure, through gender-based violence.

One of the only places today where a woman has the power to stand equal to a man is the voting booth. A power that women didn't have up until a few decades ago, across most countries in the world—with Saudi Arabia being the last country to grant this right, in 2015.

Gianna, my Italian grandmother, was one of them. Born in 1922—the year fascism entered government in Italy—she didn't gain her right to be a full citizen, to vote, until 1945, once fascism was dismantled and the current Italian constitution adopted. A right which she treated as the most precious thing on earth every time there was an election: I remember her taking out her "fancy" heels, coat, and purse for the occasion; packing her electoral card as if it was sacred; walking to the voting station to make her voice count; and then following the election results on TV in silence, seated on her large sofa chair, waiting for the final count as if it was going to determine the upcoming years of her life. "They remind me of Mussolini", she used to say each time right-wing parties won. "I lived it on my skin, and I am terrorised to see your generation forgetting what not having equal rights or a democratic society looks like".

Without voting rights, women were indeed excluded for centuries from the construction of our countries, deprived of the possibility of having their issues heard, represented, and taken forward at all levels of society. While women now have the right to vote, the reality is that, even today, many of us have to deal with attempts of control by male figures, with abuses and violence, or simply by being relegated to marginal roles—if any at all—in organisations and governments, just because we are women.

Luckily, many in this world have had the wisdom, charisma, and persistence to dedicate their lives to changing this status quo—by reminding us that things were and can again be different; by organising and empowering those around them to change the hierarchical male system rather than preserving it; and by reminding each and every one of us—woman or man—that we are all linked, not ranked. Gloria Steinem is one of them: a symbol of the women's liberation movement, a writer, and an organiser, who has touched and changed the lives of millions of women, in the US and internationally. Someone who has become so iconic that sitting in front of her feels surreal, exciting, intimidating, all at the same time.

Gloria's interview is the final one for this book. I should feel confident, in the flow, after all the previous ones went smoothly, but it's the opposite. She has already shared so much rich insight and so many learnings with the world that I don't know what else I could ask her. And speaking of women's leadership with the icon of the feminist movement, with someone who has moved mountains for gender equality, makes me feel tiny, and my book too small a drop in the ocean of change. "A drop though to which Gloria Steinem is keen to contribute to, so it must be worth something", I reassure myself as I wait for her to connect to our video call.

As soon as I see her face appear, contoured by her just as iconic blond hair bangs, I smile. Gloria smiles back warmly and waves to say hello—with her long hands and always curated nails. She is sitting at a desk in her New York home—surrounded by wooden furniture, a fireplace behind her, with a painting of a woman above it. It's a house which Gloria has had for decades but which hasn't been her true home until recently.

"It has always been an open home, filled with boxes, with people coming and going, meeting and working, since I spent my life on the road, not here", says Gloria. Writing, listening, organising, speaking: this is what she has dedicated her life to. All with one aim: encouraging, empowering, helping women achieve equal rights and opportunities, be it in a tiny village in India or on the large avenues of New York city, in the palaces of power or during the first-ever women's convention in the US.

"But I now long for a home", she adds. "During the pandemic, I took time to unpack the boxes, make it my place, from which I leave and return to from the road".

At age 89, Gloria has (at least partially) settled down, for the first time ever in her life, as her journey on the road started the moment she came into this world.

THE ROAD

Her father was a travelling antique salesman. Her mother was a journalist, who left her job to care for her two daughters and follow her husband's life on the road—up to their divorce. This set-up entailed Gloria growing up without a fixed home, changing schools or studying by herself, moving from one place to the next and discovering her country: the USA. All of this was encompassed by another unique element: her mother's belief in theosophy. A religion for which the soul of a child is not a blank page but the simple continuation of previous lives and experiences. Meaning a parent's role is not to teach, but to accompany, not to impose, but to facilitate the child's unfoldment, empowerment, to the next stage of human evolution—and this was how the Steinem daughters were raised.

"I had a peculiar childhood", admits Gloria in a serene voice, at peace with the ups and downs of it.

"My father had two points of pride: never wearing a hat, which was something you were supposed to do in his generation, and never working for someone else. He was upbeat, always searching for a new adventure, seeing solutions, never problems", she explains as I start understanding where she got those traits from. "To make a living, in summers, he ran a not very successful resort; in winter, we would hit the road to sell small antiques. From the moment I was old enough, I helped wrap and unwrap the hundreds of objects we travelled with. I was his buddy, his companion, his co-worker. I still see us standing in a little country store and me asking for a dime. 'For what?', he said. 'You can give it to me or not give it to me, but you can't ask me for what', I answered. I must have been 5. I remember looking up and hearing my father saying I was right and handing me a dime. I was his equal, always", she explains with pride in her voice.

Her expression becomes slightly thorny, as she shares the other half of her family story: "My mother, on the contrary, couldn't live the worldly life she would have hoped for. She was ill, suffered nervous breakdowns, spent a year in a sanatorium. As a teenager, I cared for her following my parents' divorce, which wasn't easy. It is during those years though that I absorbed her passion for politics, her love for writing—a love which she couldn't fulfil due to her illness but also to structural barriers women faced in society. But which she transmitted to me". Her eyes get less pensive, lighter, "I sometimes feel as if I lived her unlived life. Worldly, free, and filled with writing", she adds with a warm smile.

"It's to my parents' credit that I learned from a very young age the circularity, the equality, not the hierarchy of relations: be it unpacking antiques side by side with my father or caring for my mother when she could no longer care for me. It's to my parents' decision of not making me go to school that I owe the freedom of thought: I missed a certain amount of brainwashing, especially on gender", she says with irony in her voice. "It's to my dad's choice of living on the road that I owe the life I would have never imagined: an organiser, equipped—since childhood—with managing change and uncertainty, with the desire of being my own boss. And it's to my mother, to the personal and structural failure behind her life, that I owe what I have become: a feminist, an activist, thirsty to change the system that held back my mother and too many other women across the world".

After high school, Gloria enrolled in Smith College to study government—following in her sister's footsteps. "I felt insecure, coming from a high school whose only strength was the football team", explains Gloria with a soft laughter. "But I soon fell in love with books, with writing, and that was all I needed to keep me going". Once she graduated, it was time for what society saw as the next step: marriage. Engaged but confident that was not the right choice for her, Gloria accepted a two-year fellowship to India—postponing the wedding, which then never happened, and choosing to have an abortion while in London, where she had gone while waiting for the Indian visa. The fellowship and this set of decisions marked the rest of her life, by planting in her a deep sense of justice, equity, freedom, and by watering the seeds of activism.

ESCAPING EXPECTATIONS: INDIA AND THE ROAD AHEAD

"India had recently become independent", explains Gloria while passing her hand through her hair—to put it in order. "I spent my time travelling to villages with women who were organising other women to fight against injustice and abuse. And I learned so much. First, that change is bottom up. My mother loved the Roosevelt's and thought they had single-handedly saved us from the Great Depression—so to me, change was top down. Actually, it doesn't have to be either or", continues Gloria to clarify her point. "We need information and enlightenment wherever we find it, but we also need to be on the alert for bottom-up change and give it the credit it deserves. Even during the Great Depression, it was people cooperating with each other, creating jobs, sharing food, which saved us. This bottom-up change, which I witnessed with my eyes in India, is not what history books usually teach us. It's a neglected paradigm, which I learned in India we had to bring back to the front stage", she adds with conviction in her voice. "I also learned something else. I remember interviewing a wonderful, wise, woman, named Kamaladevi Chattopadhyay (Indian social reformer and freedom activist who played a crucial role in India's independence movement and in uplifting women by pioneering cooperation). And asking her about Gandhi's leadership. She listened to me patiently, and finally said, 'Well, my dear, we taught him everything he knows'. This is how I learned that Gandhi's leadership tactics came from the women in his family, in his country, from India's national women's movement. Even today, it is understood as a Gandhian movement and not as a women's movement, which is problematic. But discovering the real roots behind Gandhi's leadership taught me the potential and the power within women, within feminism, to change a society, to free a country".

These lessons Gloria kept alive in her own life and activism once back in the US. "I started working as a freelance journalist in New York and quickly discovered that as a woman, my writing was confined to lifestyle and fashion". Unhappy with these societal limits, Gloria started pushing boundaries. And the rest is history: she denounced the sexist working conditions of *Playboy* Bunnies after working as one of them undercover, to then help found *New York Magazine*; she started speaking up, along with a friend of hers, on women's liberation issues—disclosing her personal abortion story; then, she founded *Ms* magazine with two other colleagues, liberating female journalists once and for all from the constraints of writing exclusively about fashion and lifestyle; she co-lead demonstrations across the US to call for equal rights and co-founded the National Women's Political Caucus, supporting the election of pro-equality women to public office. She did so much, for each of us reading these pages, that it is not possible to capture it just with words. But everything she did, she did not do alone.

CO-CONSTRUCTING CHANGE

"You know . . . I started as a writer. And I have always been terrorised of speaking in public. So, when I was encouraged to do so, I knew I simply couldn't do it by myself. That's how I came to ask a friend of mine, who had a childcare centre, was the mother of three, a little younger than me and a woman of colour, to do it together. I thought women were way more likely to identify with her, given her experiences, than with me. And just like that, we started wandering around the country as a team, speaking together". As she shares this story, I can feel the excitement in her voice, of reliving that moment. "It worked tremendously well...", continues Gloria. "On top of feeling less lonely on stage, by being together, we represented a wider range of experiences than either one of us could have separately. And the moment we showed up together on stage, we could feel the relief of the audience, the confirmation that it was okay for a diverse group of people, women of colour and white women, mothers and non-mothers, lesbians and heterosexuals, to be together. By co-speaking, we exemplified something and made it happen. Of course, we are far from having achieved parity, but since then, this has been my rule while trying to fight for gender equality: to co-do with others".

Co-founding, co-leading, co-speaking. This "co-" is crucial to Gloria; it means replicating the circularity she learned from her own family; it means building on each other's strengths and supporting each other's vulnerabilities. "People say God—who always looks like a white man, by the way—is in the detail", she says with a witty expression, "and I say that the Goddess is in the connections. We are social creatures", continues Gloria without any doubt in her voice. "We need each other to sustain the energy while doing this work, and connection is what always inspired me, fuelling the engine behind everything I do". An energy which she succeeded in sustaining with depth and lightness, with urgency and patience.

As I hear her speak about the women's movement, the change that still lies ahead, the frustrations she accumulated in a lifetime, with so much calmness in her voice, I wonder how she holds these extremes together. "It's true", she says. "When you say social movement, it seems serious, difficult, urgent. But it's not only that . . . it's also about laughter—the ultimate symbol of freedom. It's about hope—because without it, we are not going to reimagine our world. It's about action, the action of each person composing the movement—otherwise a movement remains merely people moving, not changing the future. And it's about patience—change will come, but we must persist for it to happen".

All these traits are what make social justice movements a collective and positive means for change while at the same time, being a trusted messenger: such movements have on average greater credibility than political parties. "It's crucial to use that credibility wisely", explains Gloria, "and that is done not by acting on behalf of others, be it based on our interests or our assumptions of what their interests are. Rather, it is done by asking what those most impacted want and then helping them get just that".

With these words, Gloria touches a vital point: listening to empower others rather than assuming their needs to then take direct action. To her, this is the purpose and real leadership behind and within social movements: support people, expand their options of belonging to something different from what they currently belong to, while giving them the power to bring that change. "And there is one element that binds this together: trust", adds Gloria, "which is the basis of true power. If you and I have a track record together, know each other, I have come to trust you, and you tell me something, then I'll be persuaded to act with you. Because it's not power over people, but the power to act together, based on trust, that allows you to bring change". She stops for a second, as if she is savouring that feeling of trust. "That is truly irreplaceable. . .", adds Gloria with her calm and persuasive voice. "That type of power is the best option we have for sustainable and deep change. And this is why I have been interested in it throughout my life. I never thought of myself as someone wanting a job, to be a boss, much less to get elected. I never desired power over people, but power to act with others by my side—never giving up, while dancing and laughing along the way to sustain the energy. And", she says while putting her finger up as if to mark an important point, "that type of power should never be misused, if you hope to maintain it with time".

EXPANDING LEADERSHIP MODELS

While joining the wave of the feminist movement, in 1969, Gloria says it felt natural from the get-go, for herself and the other women leading the movement, to search for that type of power, to protect it from any misuse, by seeking a leadership that was communal rather than hierarchical. "We nurtured incoming leaders and future leaders. We allowed for a more elastic and inclusive style compared to the one you typically find in formal work and male-dominated environments. And we were never exclusive". Gloria uses her fingers to count how they made inclusivity a reality. "One, we included men who were feminists, be it in *Ms* magazine or in demonstrations. Two, women of colour constituted the core of it". Gloria clarifies this, as it touches on one of the greatest misconceptions behind the women's movement, a misconception created by biased press coverage: that the movement was led more by white women than by women of colour. "That's simply untrue", she explains. "It has always been the other way around. Already in the 1970s, one of the first survey on women's views showed that women of colour were twice as likely to support the movement than white women. And not because there is some difference in race, but because of a difference in situation: white women are statistically more likely, if I am not mistaken, to be dependent on the income of a white men when compared to a woman of colour. Meaning women of colour were freer and more advanced in their independence than white women, and in turn, more involved in the movement". She pulls up a third finger, for her final point: "Third, the vision and leadership often came from lesbian women, who always had the tendency to be more advanced in their consciousness. You know?", she says with a more severe tone. "A lot of women, even today, are voting in the interest of their husbands, because they are dependent on them from an income and social status perspective. That's just how it is—and that's the only way to explain women's votes for Trump: oppression works because it is internalised, and so many women around us have internalised it over generations—so much so that they can't even see it. But lesbians didn't and don't have that dependence on men, be it social or economic. And that allowed them back in the 1960s and today to be one step ahead when it comes to our emancipation from patriarchy".

Gloria's three points speak to how inclusiveness and circularity were core elements of this movement, not only its end goals. A case in point of what leading change by example looks like. "It simply can't be a feminist movement if it doesn't include all women, of all colours, of all sexual orientations" re-emphasises Gloria, while stressing once more that even if she is known as one of the most iconic faces of the movement, she was simply one of them, co-constructing and co-leading change with a diverse group of friends, of leaders.

MODESTY: WITHOUT IT, CHANGE SIMPLY CAN'T HAPPEN

As she says these words, I ask myself if I would succeed in remaining as modest as she is against the backdrop of such fame. "I suspect it was easier for me to keep that connection". I hear some hesitation in her voice, as she takes a moment to reflect, put her thoughts in order. "You know . . . it's because I'm part of a social justice movement, not a corporate or political hierarchy. This means never having had the power to tell people what to do but only having the power of our example, of leading through inspiration, through information, through persuasion. And modesty is crucial for this to work", as she explains her reasoning, the voice finds its confidence back. "Not putting yourself at the centre, but the work. Not putting your interests or assumptions ahead, but the ones of the greater group. And without modesty, capacity for listening, learning, this simply can't happen".

I share with Gloria that I wish we could see more of this model of leadership in our professional environments, in politics. "It's a model of leadership that works. It worked for so many years before patriarchy was instated, and it works still today in communities which have been immune to patriarchal change".

One example of this can be native American communities—with which Gloria shares a special connection. "I was in upstate New York just last weekend, visiting a group which has been there since time immemorial. And there was a woman, colloquially known as "Mama Bear", leading it. She is understood to be a leader without resentment from men, but with support from all—be it men and boys or women and girls. The image of leadership is seen as a maternal one, not a hierarchical one. And when you see it, you experience it on your skin—it's striking how natural it feels", says Gloria with a maternal smile.

"Such examples exist or have existed all over the world: proving it was as likely to be female leaders as male leaders, that society can be egalitarian, not patriarchal. And each of us needs to do his or her part to rediscover that balance. Because humanity is like a bird: half of it is male, let's say the right wing, and half of it is female, the left wing. And with a broken wing, which right now we still are as women, the bird simply can't fly. This goes both ways though. . ." I ask her what she means by that, as we often tend to think of women's empowerment, not of men's empowerment. "Well", she says with a sweet smile in reaction to my statement, "I can think of two things. Just as women become whole people by being active outside of the house, men become whole people by being active inside the house. By being fathers, caretakers, housecleaners. It takes both for change to happen. And just as we have begun to raise our daughters more like sons, we have not dared yet to raise our sons more like daughters—and that is a fundamental next step for real change to happen". I nod as she says these words, as it speaks to my hope behind this book: supporting men and women to lead in their own way. By opening our eyes on the diversity and variety of leadership models, by empowering women to step up the ladder, while also freeing men from being only on the ladder, and together changing the rules of the game.

"I remember so neatly", says Gloria reacting to my point, "talking to a woman—just a few years ago—who had an unusually high position in a corporation. When she got angry, she cried, which is not unusual among women: it's a kind of loss of control after holding the anger inside us for too long. This is though not understood as the style of executive behaviour", she says while looking for my confirmation as that is clearly a faraway world from her. I nod, and she continues, "And often it is not even interpreted in the right way: how often do you think 'she is angry' when you see a woman crying, and how often do you think 'she is sad, she is weak'? I bet it's usually the second one", I nod again, realising that I am myself a victim and perpetrator of that bias: I would have picked sad, not angry. At the same time, I suddenly realise that when I cry, it's because I am angry, not sad, so I sit with this internal contradiction as Gloria continues the story. "This is where this executive female leader decided to intervene, to change the paradigm. By telling those around her, her employees, her peers, 'You may think I am crying because I am sad. But no, I am crying because I am angry'. And it worked. It changed the social acceptance and perception of her tears. And that is what we must do, each in our way: shift the paradigm, not how we feel or how we express our emotions". And there is nothing more powerful than seeing executives, renown leaders, role models, doing just that—opening the opportunity of behaving differently for those to follow.

To Gloria, one of the women who most shifted the paradigm, and inspired her to do the same, was Wilma Mankiller. Elected first-ever female chief of the Cherokee Nation in 1985, Wilma was pivotal in carrying the traditions, values, and legal codes of her American-Indian tribe, in reaffirming their rights and advancing their well-being during her 10-year tenure. And she did so by showcasing virtuous governance, by focusing on education, on access to water and basic services, decreasing infant mortality, and doubling the population of her tribe—from 68,000 to 170,000.

"She is no longer with us", says Gloria as sadness appears in her eyes, "and I miss her every single day. But her leadership will always remain an example. She was nurturing, not competitive. She was a consensus builder. You felt her encouragement, the ultimate aim of fostering the leadership of others. And to me she is a proof that original cultures, before the patriarchal monotheistic Europeans showed up, embedded what we are now aspiring to: a circular and equitable leadership . . ." I see Gloria's eyes are filled with a sense of affection and admiration for her friend, her role model. "It's as if we are trying to get back to what was already here", she then adds with remorse in her voice, towards the "patriarchal monotheistic Europeans" who imposed their way of being and of leading—undermining the wisdom (on top of the rights and lives) of those who came before them.

There are so many examples of this type of leadership. So much proof that it can work. "I saw it in India, I saw it in the feminist movement, I saw it in Wilma Mankiller. And if you take the road, as I spent my life doing, you'll find infinite examples. In communities, in families, in social movements, in political parties. As I say in my book [*My Life on the Road*, 2015], travelling allows you to shift away from mere statistics and into stories, from denial into reality, from caution into action", repeats Gloria. "And as we do what we see, not what we are told, travel was for me a unique opportunity to learn by example and to lead by example. Allowing me to be fully alive in the present as hardly anything else allows you to . . . well", she adds with a witty smile, "apart from truly mutual sex, or a life-threatening emergency", and bursts into her sincere but contained, bold but modest, laughter.

WRITING, HER ULTIMATE HOME

"A life of organising", I say, "on the road". Gloria nods, but I see she gets a veil of doubt in her eyes . . . after a moment of silence, she corrects me. "I spent my life organising, and I love doing it, but I still see myself as a writer. On one hand, I am someone who hates conflict, and when you are in the public eye, conflict is difficult to avoid. Writing is my way of dealing with conflict, in a calm way—this is why it remains deeply important to me. On the other hand, I still feel something while writing that I don't feel while doing anything else—be it public speaking, be it organising, or living life. I feel as if in that moment, I am not meant to do anything else. It's where I feel calm, accomplished, at home".

As Gloria says these words, I start reflecting on my own experience. Which is similar and opposite at the same time.

I am quite sure that if you asked people around me, my partner, friends, or family, they would not define me as a conflict avoider, and some might even say I don't at all mind engaging in it when it's for the right reasons—usually finding the right and wittiest words at the right and most heated moment. But I do realise that I am heavily affected by its consequences . . . I stay awake at night (very unusual for me, as one of my golden rules to be productive and healthy is getting nine hours of sleep) thinking through what has been said. I am hurt by heated (especially if mean) comments that emerge in conflict situations, and I have come to realise this also applies to attacks or comments on social media from people I don't know. I take them to heart, feel distressed, doubt myself. But I live all of this after conflict happened—never during it. And I realise, as Gloria speaks of her relation to conflict and to writing, that writing also plays a role for me, simply at a different stage: not to avoid it, but to clear my head, put my thoughts in order, deal with its consequences in a calm way, regain my balance, my confidence, or simply articulate my shift in perspective after it.

On the other hand, contrary to Gloria, I feel as if I am not meant to do anything else not when I write, but while I act. I love solving a problem, taking concrete action to fix what I feel is wrong and help others do the same. That's what gives me Gloria's feeling of full presence and purpose, like nothing else does. Knowing though that both aspects—doing and writing—are important and different tools in my toolbox which, by leveraging wisely, can make me and any one of us a more efficient change-maker . . . just as Gloria leveraged her tools—writing and organising—to revolutionise our world.

As we are exchanging these thoughts, I look at Gloria, who has been sitting and chatting with me for now nearly an hour, and realise I am talking to her as if she was a friend, a colleague, someone from my generation. I somehow can't relate to her being one decade apart from my grandmothers' age. As much as they were, each in their own way, feminists for their time, Gloria just feels different. Dynamic, modern, avant-garde, more iconic than ever even in the sunset of her life—as Diane von Furstenberg likes to put it. And I wonder what drives her capacity to push boundaries, relentlessly, even now, a capacity which makes her a contemporary icon for women spanning over three generations.

HOPE, THE FUEL THAT KEEPS US GOING

She smiles, as she knows what the magic formula is: "I am a hope-acholic", confirms Gloria. "As most leaders in this book", I tell myself—which might explain why they kept the drive and fulfilled so many dreams and achievements in their lifetime. "At the same time, I am very aware that resistance is part of the journey, of any journey, of any progress, so you must be patient and continue moving ahead without losing that hope-acholic attitude".

Gloria highlights there are multiple stages to resistance. "If you are one woman, or one person—imagine someone from a minority—trying to bring change, then you'll face a certain type of resistance. The moment you become three, the resistance you face will evolve, it will change face. And it will shift again as you become a whole neighbourhood, or a city, or a country. Resistance is always there, it's a natural part of progress. And we can't be frightened by it, we can't be seduced into stopping or giving up because there is too much resistance. We must simply find ways of dealing with it and of protecting each other along the way". Gloria returns to this key point repeatedly: having each other, to make sure we get to the end of the way. "That's exactly the job of a movement. I can assure anyone reading these words that if you are being your authentic self, putting your body where your beliefs are, for the sake of your kids, your friends, your colleagues, then you are already part of a movement, you are already standing along others who are trying to bring similar change. And, simply by doing that, you are creating alternative support forces in the world: you are opening options for someone else—related to you or not—to have more choices of belonging . . . and that is an amazing thing to do", she says with wisdom in her eyes.

As she shares these thoughts, I can't resist asking her what the priorities should be for today's women's movement. Her modesty and organiser soul emerge again: "Well . . . it's not for me to set the priority. I should be asking you, people your age, what you feel needs changing first, and what your experience tells you of what should come next. You always start by asking. And on my side, because I am what they would have called in the 1930s a 'media worker', what I can help with is to bring attention to particular needs, to new ideas, or new ways of organising, that would be helpful to women and men in other parts of the country or of the world—for them to become more efficient change-makers".

She pauses, and probably reads in my eyes I am still looking for guidance, just as millions of women do when they read her books, watch her movie, or listen to her interviews. "Okay", she says with a soft smile, accepting with some shyness my ask. "I think the priority has been set for us. It has been set by the fact that we, as women, have wombs. And the effort to control our wombs and our birth giving is still with us, and it's still a danger to our health and freedom. Reproductive freedom, reproductive choice, safety in giving birth or in choosing not to give birth: those are still primary problems. You can see that in the struggles in my country, in what is being attempted by state legislatures to regain control over women's bodies. This means the power of government still doesn't stop at our skins and, until it does, this is by default our priority. And this would be my main wish for women, if I could make one: that each of us has control over our own physical selves, that we could not be made to have or not have children against our wishes, and that we are safe from any form of violence".

Data from the World Health Organization shows that, even today, one in every three women worldwide (i.e. over 30% of girls and women in the world) has been subjected to either physical or sexual violence, most often from their intimate partners. In my country alone, Italy, every three days on average, we hear on the news of a new feminicide—in the majority of cases, committed by intimate partners killing their girlfriends, their wives, the mothers of their children. "The best indicator to predict if a country will take on military action, be violent against other countries", explains Gloria, "is not poverty, nor religion, or degree of democracy. It's violence against females, be it girls or women, daughters or partners. This makes it extremely important to look at the microcosm of violence, not only for women and girls *per se*, but for everybody in this world . . . because until we achieve democratic families, in which equality and respect are the basic denominator between genders, we will never see truly democratic and peaceful societies".

She takes a quick break, as I am searching for my next question, but before I ask, Gloria continues sharing a second (but connected) set of priorities: "Fake laughter, fake orgasms, fake voting: as women we still have too much of a stake in men's happiness. We vote for their interests, we fake orgasms so they feel powerful, we laugh so they think they are funny. Of course, things have improved—this is one of the uses of having a long life: you remember when things were worse, and I do remember that, very well—and believe me, things were the worst", she laughs while gesturing with her hands to make the point. "But I also can't deny that there is still a long way to go for us to be free. For us to laugh only when someone is funny, to have sex only because we want pleasure, to vote for what matters to us, not to others . . . and this liberation is what we must continue fighting for, by putting our bodies where our beliefs are. And by doing anything we f**king want", I giggle as she says this, as she manages to do so with such grace that it makes it powerful, strong, yet elegant. "Yes, if I could have another wish for women of your generation is to please do anything you f**king want", she repeats, laughing. "And doing so while creating a community of other women, ready to stand with and by you in this long but crucial intergenerational march towards freedom. I can already tell, to anyone reading these words, that you have and will always have my support, and the support of many other women who have come before you and opened the road to the change you are now taking forward. But. . .", Gloria adds as an afterthought, "until we get there, remember one thing: if there is one place in the world where the most powerful equals the least powerful it is the voting booth. So go and vote: it is not the most we can do but it is the least we should do!".

BEYOND GENDER

"What is your ideal world, your ideal outcome for this long fight for equality?", I ask Gloria. "Well, what counts for me is for us to understand that we need each other. It is as simple as that: it is not about women prevailing over men, as it surely is not about men prevailing over women. Research confirms that if you put only men around the table, they will always choose the most aggressive option—even if it's wrong. And if you put only women at the table, they will choose the most conciliatory option—even if it's wrong. This is why we need each other, the diversity we bring, to make the best choices for our communities and our countries. Remember though", she continues, "the real end-goal, at least for me, would be that we succeed in working our way out of this idea of gender. We are all humans, and that is what counts".

I find Gloria's reflection on gender intriguing. Gender is usually seen as a cultural differentiation, while sex as the biological one. And as much as I agree gender is a cultural construction, I still think there are some characteristics and traits of women or of men which have been developed and "culturalised" over time because of our biology. "It's not all about the game you decide to give to your children . . . it's not that easy", a famous primatologist, Frans de Waal, had once explained to me as I was trying to wrap my head around this nurture vs. nature debate. "It is also about what a kid *does* with that game. And primates are proof that there is a biological component that we can't and shouldn't get rid of". Experiments with primates, for example, show female chimpanzees treating a leftover broom in their cage as a baby, and male chimpanzees breaking it into pieces to then throw it around as a game. Meaning it is not only the doll or the cars, it is also what a girl or a boy will do with the doll or with the car.

On the one hand, there is this natural complementarity which Gloria refers to when speaking of the decision-making process of women or men around a table. A complementarity which is richness. But at the same time, I feel there is a tension created by this same complementarity, by our diversity. A tension generated by the centuries, the millennia of discriminations we faced as women, and with which many minorities are confronted—be it due to their sexual orientation, skin colour, or ethnicity—which makes us forget that first and foremost we are all humans. A tension which transforms our complementarity into a burden, into a disadvantage, and which sometimes pushes us to wish we could simply get rid of any difference, any diversity we bring to the table, as a means to reach full gender equality.

"We're all human beings, and our shared humanity is way more important than our gender or race or class", reaffirms Gloria. "Of course, those attributes may give us a particular experience, but still. that experience is not as important as our shared humanity". She goes silent for a few seconds, and then tries to give me an example of what she means: "We both know and trust individual men or groups of men. Right?". I nod—of course I do. "They are the ones we have worked with and come to trust. And that goes for some male leaders over other male leaders. Right?". I nod again. "Well, we need to remember that. Because today, we are very fixated on these markers. We got fixated on them because our so-called 'democracy' has, over time, elevated people into power according to these markers: you are more likely to go up if you are white, if you are educated in a particular way, and if you are a man. That's true, and we must seek change whenever we can. But it remains also as true and as important to not lose track of the fact that we are each unique individuals, who can't be put into one stereotypical box (e.g. white men) we should direct our anger towards. Gender, or race, or class, or age is not as decisive as our shared humanity, and that goes both ways, because we are linked, intertwined. This is why I believe we must stop with this 'either or' perspective and start building an 'and, and' perspective: adding leadership models to the ones shaped by white men, not eliminating white men in order for us to affirm another exclusionary leadership model".

And I couldn't agree more, as we should all focus on growing the pie rather than splitting the small and broken pie we have right now. But I want to understand better what, to someone like Gloria who has worked with and for women liberation her entire life, an alternative, or an additional, leadership model to the current (male) dominant one would look like. "You know . . .", Gloria takes some time to think it through, "I am not sure . . . . It might depend on the situation because, if you think of it, we have had dictatorial females. Sure, not nearly as many as dictatorial men, but that can be explained in two ways: first, because we haven't had as many female heads of states or rulers as we have had men; second, because females are not rewarded for patriarchal dictatorial behaviour, but for empathy, so they were probably discouraged by society to follow that trend. This means it is not because physically, or biologically, or genetically it is impossible for women to be dictators, it is because of the situation and the social pressure we are all part of. And it's very important to know that it's not impossible for women to showcase dictatorial behaviours, and to be mindful of that—otherwise we will not be on the alert for negative female behaviour. An example of this is Indra Gandhi [former Prime Minister of India, between the 1960s and the 1980s]. She was sometimes problematic as a national leader, while Gandhi—who was a male human being—was not problematic. Having a woman leader doesn't mean that she necessarily reflects the best or the essence of female leadership".

"What is that essence?", I ask. "Women are probably more empathetic, more able to feel, to know the feelings of others. And that empathy, to me, is the first brick to building leadership. It produces something physical in us, oxytocin, a chemical reaction which increases with our empathy. And leadership without empathy, without oxytocin, can be painful and dangerous. But there is also the opposite risk: feeling it too much—to the point of making us ineffective. You know. . .", she continues, "there's such a thing as being empathy sick: you lose yourself in being too empathic for others. And we must be mindful as women to not fall into that trap. Forgetting about ourselves as we are taking care of everybody's else's feelings".

HOLDING HUMANITY TOGETHER

As the discussion continues, I always get more amazed by Gloria. When you are sitting in front of her, you perceive so many different things which typically would be in contradiction: she is so engaged, totally in it, mad as hell; but she is also zen, has this amazing sense of patience, and aerial view of the problems—capturing nuances and common grounds that today's society, including some parts of major social movements, are struggling to see clearly—polarised, each entrenched in its own cave of convictions and markers. "I don't want to make us patient, I want to make us impatient", states Gloria while smiling at my observation. "But I do also think that the means create the end. If we want an end which is happy and positive, for women and for men, we must make the means, the process, just like that. And, as we are fighting to reaffirm our common humanity, we must go back to our humanity by leading by example, by being honest, at every step of the way. The simple act of sitting in a circle, of telling the truth about our feelings and life experience, of being heard and of hearing someone else's truth, that's how we understand our collective truth. And that, to me is leadership. Allowing time for each person to speak, and for everyone to listen. Because leadership is a tree that grows from the bottom up, not from the top down. And that starts with the examples we set when we are physically together, by creating circularity in leadership instead of hierarchy between us—be it from men to women or from women to men". As she finishes this sentence, Gloria drops yet another precious piece of advice to help us navigate this listening and talking dynamic: "Listen more than you talk", when you are more powerful than the others in the room; "speak as much as you listen", when you are less powerful than those surrounding you—she explains.

I take note, religiously, of what Gloria just said—as I understand it has the power to become a helpful and easy mantra to guide my attitude to listening and talking in all sorts of situations, a mantra which I am far from applying as a particularly chatty and social Italian lady. I thank her for this advice, and she straight away thanks me back: "Your energy is reaching me across the ocean", she says with eyes filled with kindness, "so I want to thank you too". We spend a moment looking into each other's eyes, and then we both automatically laugh while holding the stare. "You see? I told you before", says Gloria as she is still laughing, "laughter turns out to be the one emotion that can't be compelled, it's a proof of freedom, and it connects us all".

REGRETS

Before letting Gloria go, I have one final question I realise we have not yet touched upon: failure. And I am, once again, surprised by her reaction. "At my age, I speak of regrets, not of failures. Failures make you grow—regrets often keep you stuck. I have had misunderstandings in my life, which I find painful. You are left with the feeling that if only you could be understood, you would have a chance to explain, or something. . ." Gloria's eyes for the first time look down, "Well, it's so difficult, right?", she says. "Of course, there is some opportunity to go back and repair, and I tried to repair where I could . . . but unrepaired misunderstandings are a regret for me. The greatest regret though is not having written enough". She looks away from the screen again, as if she is processing or feeling these regrets and needs a moment to herself. "You can probably relate to this, as a writer", she continues, "but once you have missed the window of opportunity, once you have not written something you should have written at a specific moment, out of the spontaneity of experience, it isn't as if you can go back and write the exact same thing: what you would have written five years ago in a particular situation can't be written five years later. And often I don't take that time to write out of the spontaneity of experience, and that is a deep regret. A regret which becomes heavier now that I look at the time I have left". Her eyes get lighter, the wittiness returns, "I have done some research and found the oldest woman in the world was 130 . . . I mean, I'm way older than I ever thought I would be, however, realistically speaking, I don't think I will make it to 130—I wish I could though. And this saddens me, the amount of time that is left, which is surprising and regretful at the same time".

We sit for a moment with Gloria's words. I feel what she feels. Despite being two generations younger, and thereby far from those type of reflections, I have been acutely aware of the limited time we each have as a living being since I was a small kid. Perhaps because I was brought up as an atheist, not believing there is anything that awaits me after earth makes this time here even more precious, more urgent. "Well, that doesn't sound too bad to me", says Gloria with irony in her voice. "Religion is politics in the sky, of which we are not supposed to talk about—even if we should. And, what a coincidence, God looks like the ruling class, Jesus is blond with blue eyes . . . just as my parents avoided me some brainwashing by not attending schools, your parents avoided you some brainwashing by educating you as an atheist".

I agree with her and am forever thankful to my parents for not imposing a myth or personal belief on me—gifting me a freedom I would have otherwise not had. But that didn't make my fear of death any lighter. I remember, as a kid, the night before my birthdays, I would never be able to sleep. Spending hours in my bed thinking of everything I have done the previous year, of everything I wanted to do the next year, and counting down time to my old age, scared of death, and of not having enough time to fulfil all my dreams and wish lists. I remember writing in my diary I didn't want to get older, closer to death. Writing down repeatedly the number 7, or 8, or 9, of the age I was leaving in a few hours, because I didn't want to let go of that time. Making me live each birthday, yes, as a moment of celebration, because I love being celebrated and even more receiving gifts and eating sweets, but also as a moment of reflection, of fear, of nostalgia for what I have not yet done. "We can't control what happens", says Gloria to reassure, "but we can use what happens within the time we have. I don't regret how I used it, and I am intending on using this time up to the very final moment of my life, who knows, maybe it's 130"—she laughs—"by doing more of what I can uniquely do, more of what I care about, and by encouraging people like you and like those reading my words to do just the same—this is how you create circularity, and this is what our world needs".

I thank Gloria again, for everything she has done, she is doing, and she will do until she reaches 130. Feeling we will never be able to thank her, and all the women who stood with and by her for our collective liberation enough. She thanks me back, with her usual modesty, and we wave goodbye. She bends her hands together, as a "namaste"; I do the same, while one of her staff appears on screen to help her hang up from the call—and, just like that, she is gone again.

As I stand up from my desk, I still feel the nervousness I had
before starting the call. I feel moved from everything she has
just said. In awe of her work, of her strength, of her kindness.
And still caught in a moment of surrealism, between reality and
dreaming. I started this book worrying who would accept being
part of it—I finish it by interviewing the icon embedding all
this book stands for—and I struggle to believe it. I feel happy
to have had this time with her and sad it is already over. I feel
worried I didn't ask everything I would have wanted to, excited
of writing everything down, concerned I won't do her justice.

But in the midst of all these emotions, of one thing I feel reassured: that that's OK. That we can be happy and pissed, understanding and impatient, confused and determined, filled with
self-doubt and self-confidence, allies of men and true feminists.
Because holding nuances, diverse feelings, and speaking the
truth behind them is what makes us grow, learn, listen, lead.
It is what makes us humans, above all. And this is the example,
the legacy, that Gloria is leaving us with: doing whatever the
f**k we want, while being true to ourselves, kind to others, and
honest about it all along every step of the way.

CONCLUSION: IT STARTS WITH EMPATHY

WRITING THIS BOOK HAS been an unforgettable journey.

I got to meet, debate, learn from, and learn with trailblazing women. Women who confided in me their stories, their failures, their fears, their hopes, their vision for a different and better world.

And putting it into words, bringing it all together, trying to do it justice was no easy task.

To get started, it required *optimism*: believing that such a project should and could become reality, believing that impressive women would take time to speak to me, not to shine, but to question and explore their journeys and redefine leadership models while doing so. Once in it, it required *curiosity*, meaning the capacity to listen, uncover, discover others, and then create something innovative with all I had collected through hours of chats between Paris, London, Brussels, New York, Denver and Istanbul. Listening not to judge, not to respond, but to understand, to learn—which I once again realised is not as easy as it seems, in an era where we often talk to share our story rather than to learn from others, where we debate to be right, to prevail, rather than to understand different perspectives. And it required more *consistency* than I thought it would: putting my energy and bringing my ambition to the table at every step of the way, in each email, in each interview, in each follow-up comment, after each "no", each obstacle, each challenge. Making sure that despite the setbacks, I would continue moving forward and not get discouraged by the problems along the way.

It consisted in a real proof of *freedom*, of being able to say what needs to be said, not what others want to hear. The freedom of speaking up to power, to old-style schemes, and to ingrained system flaws which we together hope to change—even a tiny bit—through the pages of this book and through the seeds of reflection and action we have planted in each person reading this. It required *integrity*, being clear on the principles and the philosophy guiding this book and sticking to it. This sometimes required putting my foot down—not the easiest thing to do when you have in front of you leaders of such stature—but together we kept the honesty and the sincerity behind each word you have read.

It required *authenticity*, a lot of it. Because authenticity creates more authenticity, and there is simply no way around that. In this book, you find my complete and honest self, with my ups and downs along the way. And you find it because that's who I am, but also because I am convinced that you can't expect authenticity from others without giving it first. These leaders related to me, to the project, and decided to share difficult parts of their journeys just as I was sharing mine with them. And I hope, in turn, that their authenticity has allowed many of you to relate to them—not because of what they have done, because of their successes, but because of who they are: humans, above all, with strengths, vulnerabilities and doubts, just like yours and mine. Which also means anyone of us can become today's or tomorrow's trailblazers, do things differently, just as these women have—because it doesn't require superpowers, it simply requires being yourself, following your passions and working hard to pursue your goals. Further, it required *circularity*. Sitting together, as peers, sharing our own truth to build together a bigger truth—which can guide our vision and actions to shape what leadership means and, through that, shape our world for the years to come.

It required, in a way, *leadership*—in keeping an eye on the end-goal and vision while managing successes and failures along the way; in building a process (with each one of the incredible persons involved) capable of reflecting and exemplifying the outcome: a different way of working, of thinking, of relating to each other, of supporting each other—with the hope to, in turn, see these shifts more and more infused into the world outside of the pages of this book.

But what it required, most of all, is something we have encountered throughout the lines of this book, through the words and anecdotes of these leaders, but have not named explicitly: *empathy*. Feeling with someone, understanding their viewpoint, their personal story, their thinking, their sensitivities and fears, to create a bold, ambitious, vulnerable, honest final result, which hopefully holds the power to make us think and act differently. It required the same empathy which all the women interviewed for this book display in managing their teams, companies, international negotiations, and that allows them to continuously innovate and solve our worlds' problems—while inspiring others to do the same.

Empathy is indeed the first and final building block of leadership, with—in the middle—the traits and skills (among others) we uncovered in this book. A building block which is not just a "nice to have" but a "must have". "Leadership without empathy can become dangerous"—Gloria Steinem reminded us. And it's enough to take a quick look at the daily news, no matter where we live, to find extensive examples of the consequences of leadership without empathy.

It is indeed no coincidence that today's world is facing a combination of unprecedented crises. Crises which you are seeing and feeling in your own life: poverty and economic recession; pandemic; the shrinking space for democratic participation coupled with the deepening polarisation within and across our countries, communities, families; the discrimination of minorities, be it of individuals part of the LGBTQI+ community, of ethnic minorities, of religious minorities; the inequality between genders, social classes; climate change, loss of biodiversity and increasingly extreme weather events affecting us all.

Crises which, more often than not, result into conflict. Wars are raging in too many villages, cities, countries, and continents. In the twentieth century alone, an estimated 108 million people have been killed in conflicts. And currently, there are over 100 active conflicts in the world, with over two billion people—i.e. one-fourth of humanity—living in areas affected by these wars.

There is, though, a silver lining: all these crises, from wars to poverty, from climate change to inequalities, are human made (or, some would argue, man-made). And just as we made them, it's possible to unmake them—and that depends entirely on us.

How? It starts with adding the element which we have for too long dismissed in leadership: empathy, as the central building block to create a leadership capable of addressing and solving these crises.

This capacity to feel and to know the feelings of others is often perceived as a more feminine trait. We can't know how much of it is nature, how much of it is nurture, but experts confirm a greater inclination towards empathy among women. Research indicates that women are more prone to think long-term, to lead with competence and empathy, to act in the interest of others, of everyone, not only their own. And facts prove it: women leading countries and companies are creating more high-performant, functional, fair, and sustainable societies and organisations. Countries led by women showed innovative trust-based communication and leadership styles while managing the COVID-19 pandemic—which helped limit the spread of the virus and reduce death rates. And today, in the face of the war between Russia and Ukraine, of the protests in Iran, of the war in Yemen or in Ethiopia, we can't not ask ourselves if history would have unfolded itself in the same way if power had been held also by women.

There might be a biological component to it, as matriarchs and mothers care for others—as also observed among primates by primatologists such as Frans de Waal. There surely is a cultural component to it, as socially, girls and women tend to be rewarded for being relational, empathetic, docile, while boys and men tend to be rewarded for being competitive, assertive, focused on their self-interest. No matter the reason behind this predisposition women have towards empathy, it remains a trait our world is desperately in need. A trait which—as women and as men, as girls and boys—we should and could bring much more to the table, to lead in a different way. And we should do so always more—not less, as we climb up the ladder, as we reach the highest levels of responsibility, of power, of leadership, as these levels enable us to have the highest reach and impact on other people's lives—and, without empathy and connection, we risk doing more harm than good.

It is undeniable that the dominant leadership style, defined over the centuries by and for men, has proven to no longer be fit-for-purpose for what our world needs right now—meaning we have reached a stage where we must question the "normal way" of doing things. A stage in which we much imagine and foster a new style of leadership, capable of addressing and solving the imminent global challenges we are confronted with.

A leadership focused on protecting and promoting the common good, on sustainability, fairness, equity. Capable of long-term thinking and immediate and effective action, to catalyse short- and long-term change. Of holding together and managing complexity—using both rationality and empathy. Of leading in a bold yet kind way, showing the example and bringing people together around common values, visions, and actions—halting the increasing polarisation and divisions we are witnessing in our communities and countries.

A leadership which must be undertaken by women and men alike, interrupting the broken schemes and the unhealthy gender-based and gender-biased social reward mechanisms—constraining women and men, boys and girls, while putting back at the centre what really counts: not profit, not success, not power, not ego; but our collective well-being, for us today, for the generations to come, and for the planet overall.

A leadership which is no longer a simple synonym of authority, of power over people, but of inspiration, of example, of power to act, to bring change, inspiring others to take responsibility and act along you.

A shift that starts with a question: *why?* Why do the leaders in this book, I, you, want to lead? By asking this question and by being driven by this *why*, this purpose, we can transform leadership into the power of creating and reaching common objectives, driven by a common purpose, by a sense of shared belonging and responsibility. Managing to do just that is what leadership should be about. What leaders should stand for.

The first good news is that anyone, no matter the gender, age, or background, can be that leader, bring that change, within our family, our schools, our workplaces, our communities, our nations. This shift in leadership needs to come both from the bottom and from the top for change to happen, and to happen fast, and we need each of you as part of this change.

The second good news is that the lessons and insights gathered in this book can hopefully give any of us a jump start for implementing a new way of leading, in *our* way, regardless of whether we are a top executive, a student, a teacher, an organiser, an employee, a politician—because you can lead from wherever you are.

Through these interviews, I, myself got to challenge and refine my own thinking as a CEO, as a leader and as a woman, of what leadership means to me, and of how it should evolve if we want to fix our world. And I now want to share my takeaways with you, with the hope you can treasure some of these insights and use them as a guide in every step of your leadership journey, and of life.

BE YOURSELF AND BE HAPPY ALONG THE WAY!

Being ourselves is our secret superpower—because that is what makes us unique. As a person to whom it comes naturally to be spontaneous and confident about who I am and what I stand for, I always had a feeling that this authenticity was part of what helped me emerge in my career, but my encounters with these leaders confirmed it. By owning their strengths and their vulnerabilities, by speaking their mind and following their intuition, by being curious and daring to think out of the box, by following their passion and not what they were expected to do, these leaders built over time an edge—which allowed them to change what they wanted to change and get where they wanted to be.

Just as these leaders appear in these pages, at times successful and at times lost, at times sad and at times happy, at times incredibly smart and at times insecure, each of us is multidimensional, and that is the beauty of humanity. The reality though is that many of us are taught to hide the dimensions that make us seem different, thinking that 'fitting in' or 'faking it' makes our life easier. Owning these different dimensions, not hiding them, is the way to go—as these leaders show us. It's a path which unlocks a potential we didn't think to hold within us. A path which will give you that edge, that passion, that instinct to inspire others and to do things differently, bringing your uniqueness to the table, not keeping it under wraps.

But, more importantly, it's a path that will make you happy, at ease, truthful to who you are—not to who or what others want you to be like. We can learn this from Diane von Furstenberg who reminds us that "authenticity is the best chance and path we've got to be happy, to get and sustain energy throughout our time on earth, while trying to leave something better behind"!

DARE, FAIL, AND START AGAIN. . .

It takes courage to dare, to fail, and even more courage to then start again. But that courage will take you far. The leaders in this book share this courage. And they share one clear approach to life: failures are necessary steps to success, and we should start seeing them not as setbacks but as a way of redirecting our energy and purpose, as opportunities to learn and do better the next time around. As difficult as it might sound, also to me as I am writing these words, the truth is that we shouldn't be scared to fail, but prepared to fail, expecting that to happen, and being ready to readjust once it does.

Being curious, innovative, making mistakes, failing, getting back on our feet, and learning from it all is something we should overall re-evaluate as a society. Gitanjali Rao urges us to start by teaching this in our schools if we hope to foster the next generation of leaders capable of fixing global challenges. Fostering innovation, fostering new ways of thinking, of living, of acting, of failing and succeeding, is the only way we've got to create a different-looking world—and trial and error are a core and natural part of it. And this is valid no matter our age!

REBOOT: BY LISTENING RATHER THAN SPEAKING

As I write this paragraph, I realise I must preface it by admitting I am not great at this. Not great at all. Like many others, I speak more than I listen, I know more than I learn, and I affirm more than I ask.

The reality though is that anyone, in order to be an effective change-maker, needs to be able to listen, to understand the context, the people we are trying to help. Because learning happens throughout our life cycle and, if it doesn't, we stay stuck in the past.

The stories in this book confirm how crucial that is. Tawakkol Karman led a revolution by listening to her people, organising and standing with them to call for change. Christiana Figueres gave, for the first time in history, a central role to civil society and representatives from a broad range of under-represented groups as part of the climate change negotiations, listening to their needs and to their experiences—and learning from them, to then incorporate these learnings in the governmental process. Becky Sauerbrunn leads by listening to her teammates, and then creating a strategy with the best ideas that have collectively emerged.

Leaving space for others to talk, and for us to listen, is key. For this, we need to continue reminding ourselves that the more we go up, the more we should listen, if we hope to be effective and inspiring leaders.

PATIENCE AND URGENCY—TWO SIDES OF THE SAME COIN

Another common trait which emerged through the pages of this book is something which is hard to do but which can become pivotal for a revised interpretation of leadership: the art of dealing with, working on, advancing at the same time what is important and what is urgent, long-term and short-term priorities.

What is important is usually never seen as urgent, while what is urgent is often not that important in the long run. Think of climate change: scientists, students have been ringing the alarm bell for decades now but—despite its importance—even today it is not an urgent item on most government agendas, unless there is an immediate climate-related emergency they need to deal with. This is just one proof of the fact that by not addressing what is important, we transform it into an urgency, an emergency, for people coming after us. As Comfort Ero shared in her interview, prevention is better than cure—and it is by far the most cost-effective (and lifesaving) approach.

We are all drawn to what is urgent rather than to what is important, and we can observe it in our daily lives. How much time do you spend responding to emails and messages, just because you are solicited, rather than working on what would be important and would make a difference in the long run? How much time do you spend finishing up small tasks rather than spending quality time with someone important? This is why managing to combine these two (sometimes contradictory) components is a real art, an art which is necessary to lead us in a better direction. By responding to the urgency, while moving us in the direction of what is important—for us and for future generations.

We need leaders capable of doing just that. Just as much as we need mechanisms and incentives geared towards encouraging those in leadership positions to look, with urgency, also at what is important in the long run, going beyond short-term mandates and priorities by which heads of states, CEOs, and managers are in most cases judged and evaluated upon.

NUANCES ARE THE REAL DEAL, NOT
BLACK-AND-WHITE THINKING

The capacity to hold together urgency and patience also relates to another trait, which the featured leaders bring to the table. You might have noticed, but none of them have simplistic black-and-white views about the world—which is by now uncommon, as proven by the often polarised and polarising leaders and public discourse in many of our countries.

This shows, for example, in their conception of feminism—often (wrongly) perceived by non-feminists as a movement which is black and white. These women leaders all stress the importance of understanding that feminism has nothing to do with being against men, or with affirming women as superior to others. If you read through the lines of the book, you realise just how nuanced (and advanced) the views of these women leaders are. They see us for what we are: individuals, humans, some good, some less good—be it men or women. They look forward, not backwards, to build—women and men together—a different model of society and of leadership. Emphasising that real progress is about equality but that real progress happens when you can take people with you, not disenfranchise them along the way and, by doing so, creating more divisions and polarisation within our already divided communities and world.

To be effective leaders, we must also be bridges. Capable of seeing the reality, while aiming for the ideal. Ready to bridge the forces pushing for change with the ones resisting it, by persuading them, by seducing them—as Diane von Furstenberg likes saying—along the way. Because the real goal is to reach that endpoint together. . . as, until we are all there, there will always be strong resentful forces feeling left behind and waiting for the right moment to pull us back, as much as they can.

So true leadership must also deal with this: by understanding different perspectives, by holding the complexity of nuances and not falling into simplistic traps, trying to bridge differences and fears rather than fuelling them, recentring the people we lead, serve, around our shared humanity, our shared objectives, not around divisive markers.

THE POWER IS IN THE RELATIONSHIP WITH OURSELVES

All of this, though, is placed in one very basic but important-to-remember truth. You, I, these leaders, none of us can control all situations—what happens in our lives, in our jobs, in our family, in our world. Some parts we can influence, of course, some we can even change, and we must do so whenever possible. But we should also accept that some things are just out of our control. Be it the weather during the match for Becky Sauerbrunn and her team, be it an injury which simply doesn't recover as fast as needed to qualify for the World Cup squad.

And when that happens, we must remain flexible, readjust our strategy and priorities along the way, while keeping in sight our end-goal—where we want to go, who we want to be, why we are doing what we are doing.

And while doing so, we must remember that the one thing we truly have control over, fully and always, is ourselves. It is how we show up every day, how we build our lives, how we overcome problems.

This means it is crucial to invest in the relationship with ourselves, before investing in the relationship with the rest of the world, if we hope to be fair and inspiring leaders to others. Because it always starts with us. From building "complicity" with ourselves and remembering—while we move up or fall down the ladder of life—that we are in it for a marathon, not a sprint, and we must try and get to the end in one piece. Looking backwards and feeling we have lived fully, that we "lived 350 years" as Diane von Furstenberg says, and that we have tried to change what we could along the way, all while taking care of ourselves and those around us.

Without that solid core, that self-care, that self-kindness, we are not going to be effective in bringing change. It goes back to the strong back and the soft front Christiana Figueres speaks about, without which we will struggle to build healthy relationships in the outside world and will not be capable of inspiring others by example. Without this, we won't truly and freely be leading our way.

OVER TO YOU:

By keeping in sight all the above, centring it in our capacity to have and show empathy, in our shared humanity, we can collectively change a society, a culture, the definition of the word "leadership". By each of us showing up, doing our part, and doing it in our own way.

So now, we pass it over to you:

Why do you want to lead?
To which purposes do you want to dedicate your life?
How will you show up every day, to be the change you want to see?
How will you bring change, while planting forward for all those who will stand on your shoulders?
In short, how will you lead, in your own way?

INDEX